Horizons

Preschool Readiness

Horizons

Preschool Readiness

by
Mary Ellen Quint, Ph. D.

Designed and Edited by
David J. Korecki

Illustrated by
Tye A. Rausch

Editorial Staff
Sareta A. Cummins
Christine A. Korecki

Alpha Omega Publications
Chandler, Arizona

Preschool Readiness
Copyright © 1992 &1998 by
Alpha Omega Publications
300 N McKemy Ave, Chandler, Arizona 85226

Printed in the United States of America
ISBN #1-58095-988-1
Item # PE 4020

TABLE OF CONTENTS

Section 5–Matching and Grouping

Advanced Preschool

Section 6–Language Readiness

Section 7–Math Readiness

Materials List

PREFACE

The big question is when, how, and what to teach children?

Two completely opposite positions are currently held concerning the proper age to begin teaching children. Each of these positions contains its own method of teaching, including what to teach and how to teach. As with any unproven, dogmatic opinion, these positions have both become extreme, intolerant, and inflexible.

One of these positions is the Super Baby or the create-a-child-prodigy view of educating children. It begins before birth and often results in an almost obsessive desire on the part of parents to teach their children everything they can as rapidly as possible. This imbalanced viewpoint, that the learning of knowledge is all important, may indeed produce some child prodigies for their parents. However, some parents' pride can reach inordinate extremes in an effort to make their children special. This high pressure approach can be detrimental to a child emotionally and psychologically.

The other position is generally called Delayed Education. This equally extreme position maintains that a child should not be formally taught any academics, such as reading, writing, arithmetic, or music, until at least the age of eight and then only if the child himself wants to learn. The advocates of this viewpoint believe education should be child-centered and pressure free. They are against any rote drill, memorization, and most testing. The only education recommended under this viewpoint is that which comes from the child's play or his personal experimentation. Learning to read is actually withheld from even the inquisitive child until he is at least eight years of age. Children who possess low motivation or who have less than average intelligence can suffer long-range damage from this approach.

Is there an answer to the question "When, how, and what should I teach my children?" The answer is to know your own children and to use common sense. This book has been written to give general information about preschool children, what they can learn, and how parents can guide them in learning during their formative years. The parent is then responsible to evaluate this information and to match its use with their unique child.

Parents need to realize that they are teaching their child constantly from the moment of birth. A baby watches and learns to mimic what he sees around him. He hears when you talk, sing, and read to him. He responds to your touch, your voice, and your emotions. Parents are absolutely the most important influence in a child's development for the first five or six years. Snatches of supposed "quality time" are no substitute for the constant companionship of a mother during these highly developmental years.

Of course, there is more to child rearing than companionship. Parents also need to know what else children really need. Probably the most important thing to know about your children is that structure is needed as a normal part of their life. Newborns need the security of being fed on schedule as well as regular nap and bed times. Children also need to understand that the world does not revolve around them and that they will not get what they want just because they want it. Establishing structure for, and control over, your children is the first step toward their education.

The second most important thing to know about your children is that they know less than you do. Therefore, you are qualified to start their education. You know shapes, colors, sizes, letters, sounds, mathematical symbols, and all kinds of things they need to learn. And, you can teach them everything they need to know in order to excel later in any formal school. You may even choose to continue teaching your children at home, as so many other parents are now doing.

I am sure that this book will provide much helpful information, to add to your own common sense, which will assist you in successfully beginning your children's education.

Alan Christopherson
VicePresident, Alpha Omega Publications, Inc.

INTRODUCTION

Learning is an adventure for young children. The concepts which will be needed later for understanding academic subjects such as reading, math, and science can be learned easily and effortlessly from the world in which your children live. Everything has color, shape, size, and a relationship to the things or people about it. An awareness of this order is the beginning of learning readiness for children.

Children become interested in their immediate environment long before they walk or talk. Colors, shapes, sizes, and sounds (including language) are part of an infant's world. Often one of the first questions children will ask is "Dat?" or "Wat's Dat?" ("What's that?") as they eagerly point to both familiar and unfamiliar things. These questions need to be answered with simple, concise answers.

Parents and teachers should create surroundings for children which will stimulate their imagination. Their playrooms or play areas should contain bright pictures, mobiles, and other things which will interest children. As they grow older, you can hang the things which they make themselves in these areas.

Helping the children explore their world through reading, answering questions, and asking further questions are also important tasks for parents and teachers. This book presents many opportunities to stimulate a child's thinking and learning.

Parents and preschool teachers need to understand that children do not mature at the same rate. Just as one little boy can be 6" taller than another boy of the same age, they may drastically vary in emotional and mental growth as well. Don't be surprised if your four-year-old daughter rushes through some of the advanced activities in this book ahead of your six-year-old son. That is normal, just as are the differences in physical development between children. In fact, chronological age *cannot* be used to determine readiness any more than height, weight, or shoe size.

Your goal is not to move through this preschool program quickly, but to proceed step-by-step as the children are ready. Children should not necessarily move through these concepts in any given period of time. When this book is used with very young children, they will progress slowly. Older children may move more quickly. Basically, the concepts contained in this material should be mastered by the time children are ready to begin a formal kindergarten program. That time can be anywhere between four to six years old depending on the child's natural development and the amount of time his parents have worked with him.

About the Program

A Note to Parents: For parents who are working with their preschoolers at home, this program should provide a solid basis for kindergarten preparation. Your home, yard, city, state, church, field trips, nature walks, and grocery stores are your classroom. Each of these stages is naturally filled with materials that can be used to help your children learn. The opportunities are endless.

A Note to Teachers: For preschool teachers, this program should provide ideas for centers, learning activities, and games to be used in small groups to lead children to the readiness needed for kindergarten. Your classroom and school yard also contain a wealth of learning materials. Other materials can be requested from parents, if necessary.

Materials: Both parents and teachers are limited only by the extent of their own imaginations. Materials should be of no great expense. Most materials are readily found in the home or classroom and can be gathered in a short period of time. For those who want to purchase materials, many good items are available at local teacher-supply stores, at quality children's toy stores, in department and grocery stores, or through mail order from the publisher of this book, Alpha Omega Publications. Suggested materials are found on pages 199 to 201.

Many of the activities, games, and books suggested in this program can be used with several sections in this book. Keep in mind that the instructions given are ideas and suggestions only. We hope they will spur you on to your own ideas for further activities that will reinforce the concepts presented. If you find a game or activity that your child likes and wants to repeat, feel free to adapt the game to other new concepts in later sections. If the children think of a new activity or a game to expand an idea, *use it.*

Eye-hand Coordination: Eye-hand coordination is extremely important to develop at the preschool stage. Therefore, activities are included in every section of this book which will aid in that development.

Activities that involve tracing simple shapes, objects, paths, and mazes are coordination exercises. Little ones can use their fingers or large crayons to trace circles, squares, large pictures in coloring books, or dot-to-dot patterns. Older children can begin to use pencils, crayons, chalk, or markers to trace large numbers and letters in preparation for writing. Cutting activities, which involve cutting along defined lines, are also good eye-hand activities when children are able to handle scissors easily and safely.

Using this Program

1. First, read the short introductions to all seven sections; pages 15, 43, 73, 103, 151, 169, and 183. This will acquaint you with all the topics to be covered.

2. Activities within a section are progressive. Therefore, the earlier activities are meant for younger children. As the section progresses the activities become more difficult so that the latter activities are meant for older preschoolers.

This program is not meant to be followed by beginning at Section One, Activity One and proceeding through every single activity until reaching the end of the book. Actually, you can use any activity in any section you choose, if your child can understand the directions and is able to follow them. However, you will probably find an advantage in following a simple chronology.

3. Start reading through the activities in Section One until you reach one or two that you believe would be too difficult for your child. Then determine how far back you need to go in the activities before they would be too simple for your child. In between the "too easy" and "too difficult" activities is where your child should start. Mark as your starting place the first activity you determine is not too easy. Perform the same evaluation on each of the other six sections. (Note that Sections Four and Five are more difficult

and Sections Six and Seven even more so.) You will find few activities for a three or four-year-old in the final two sections, but reading their introductions and reviewing the activities will familiarize you with where we are going.

4. Let's assume you have a child whom you have decided can start on Section One, Activity 8; Section Two, Activity 6; Section Three, Activity 6; and Activity 1 on Sections Four and Five. You found Sections Six and Seven too difficult for now, but plan to read to your child daily to better prepare him for later.

You can now begin with the activities you marked in any section and move back and forth between sections, or progress in a single section as desired. You can even drop back to an easier activity or try a more difficult activity for interest. Continue selecting those activities which suit the needs and abilities of your children, even skipping some activities if you wish.

5. When beginning any activity, stay with it until the child either learns the lesson or tires of it. If he is having difficulty even after trying hard, stop the activity and go on to something different. Return to the difficult activity later when he is ready to try again. No time limit should be set on any activity.

6. *Repetition*: In this text certain key points are repeated, sometimes in every section. This is done to emphasize the importance of the ideas and to assist the parent and teacher so that they do not have to return to the introduction constantly to find what is considered important.

Certain activities and games are also repeated and cross-referenced when helpful in more than one area.

In the early part of the first three sections, certain types of activities are repeated to emphasize that these activities may be used together.

Some Important Points to Remember

Read, Read, Read to your children!

Answer the all important "What's that?" questions. Always speak in complete sentences even with very young children.

Talk in precise language, not in "baby talk."

Let children develop at their own pace.

Summary

The concepts covered in each section do not occur in isolation from each other. Areas and activities will overlap. Therefore, when answering a child's question or describing an object, discuss all the properties, not just those being covered in that section. When describing a ball in the color section, do not simply say, "The ball is red." But add other properties, "The ball is round." "The ball is big." "The ball is bigger than (or smaller than) _____." This type of discussion prepares the children for the sections on shape, size, and comparison of objects.

While all children are different, they normally learn first through their senses. The more senses used to experience an object, a person, or an event, the more quickly and completely a lesson can be learned. Help them to see, hear, touch, smell, and (if safe) taste. As the children grow older, make sure that they see, hear, say, trace or write when appropriate.

This program is intended to be for academic preparation solely. It is not the purpose of this program to rectify any developmental deficiencies a child might have, although many of the activities will assist development as a matter of course.

If there are any questions about the normal development of your children, we present the following general guidelines from *Growing Child* magazine. Read through the guidelines. If your children seem to be many months or even a year behind the guidelines, check with your doctor. If they are slightly ahead or slightly behind, do not worry. Remember, all children develop at their own pace.

Please write the publisher with any comments or suggestions you might have. We would enjoy knowing how your children have benefited from the use of this program.

DEVELOPMENTAL CHECK LISTS

The following six charts depict the typical development of average children brought up without specialized training, but with the normal attention of a mother and a normal family life. These charts were developed after countless hours of scientific observation by the staff at *Growing Child*. It is by their gracious permission that these charts have been reproduced here (Copyright 1982 *Growing Child* 22 North Second Street Lafayette, Indiana 47902). Any parent desiring highly creative materials written at precise development levels by the month should subscribe to:

Growing Child
22 North Second Street
Lafayette, Indiana 47902
1 (800) 927-7289
www.growingchild.com

CAUTION: *Growing Child* makes this important statement on all of their Developmental Check Lists:

"These milestones are guidelines only. All babies do not develop at the same speed, nor do they spend the same amount of time at each stage of their development. Usually a baby is ahead in some areas, behind in others and "typical" in still other areas. The concept of the "typical" child describes the characteristics one would expect to find at a given age."

In a discussion with Nancy Kleckner of *Growing Child*, she said:

"A child from a deprived home would likely be behind in his development while that same child could advance in many concepts with care. Of course, a child who has certain physical defects would also not measure as 'typical.'"

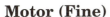

Growing Child 12 MONTHS

Developmental Check List

Social and Emotional

Gives objects on request.
Imitates hand and face gestures such as waving "bye-bye," clapping hands, closing eyes.
Helps with dressing by putting arms out for sleeves and feet for shoes.
Seeks and finds hidden toys easily.
Is affectionate toward familiar people.

Motor (Fine)

Holds spoon but needs help with its use.
Puts blocks in and out of a small box.
Uses pincer grasp (thumb and index finger) to pick up small objects or pieces of food.
Points with index finger toward desired objects.
Uses both hands freely but may demonstrate a preference for one.

Motor (Gross)

Pulls to standing position and lets self down by holding on to furniture.
May stand alone for a few seconds.
Sits well for an indefinite period of time.
May creep on all 4's.
May walk independently.

Communication

Imitates adult's playful sound making.
Recognizes own name and turns to speaker when hearing it.
Follows simple directions: "Give it to Mommy." "Come to Daddy." "Clap hands."
Babbles a lot with rhythm and variations in pitch.

Vision

Recognizes familiar people at a distance of 20 feet or more.
Watches intently small toys that are pulled across the floor at a distance of 10 feet away.

Developmental Check List

Social and Emotional
Raises and holds cup with two hands.
Drinks from a cup without spilling.
Removes shoes, socks, cap.
Imitates familiar actions such as sweeping floor, dusting, reading a book.
Amuses self, but prefers to be near an adult.
Alternates between independence and dependence on caregiver.

Motor (Fine)
Scribbles with a crayon on paper.
Can build a tower with three blocks after a demonstration.
Picks up very small objects and food immediately on sight.
Explores objects more frequently with hands than mouth.

Motor (Gross)
Pushes and pulls large objects.
Walks but with feet slightly apart.
Can do two things at once – carry a large object and walk with it.
Climbs into a large chair, rotates body, and sits in it.
May creep backward when going down stairs.

Communication
Speaks 6 to 20 recognizable words.
Likes nursery rhymes and joins in.
Echoes the last word spoken to him/ her.
"Talks" to self while playing.
Enjoys picture books.
May point to 2 or 3 parts (eyes, nose, hair, shoes) on doll or self.

Vision
Fixes eyes on and recovers a rolling ball 10 feet away.
Points to distant objects out of doors.

Growing Child 24 MONTHS

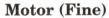

Developmental Check List

Social and Emotional
Uses a spoon to feed self.
Chews food well.
Raises and drinks from cup, then replaces it on table.
Is very possessive about toys – no sharing.
Plays beside but not with other children.
Clings to caregiver when tired or afraid.
Goes into tantrums when frustrated but can be distracted readily.
Demands a lot of caregiver's attention.

Motor (Fine)
Removes wrapper from a cupcake or candy bar.
Builds a tower of 6 blocks.
Imitates a vertical line with a crayon on paper.
Turns pages in a book one at a time.
Picks up tiny objects as small as a crumb.

Motor (Gross)
Runs on whole foot, but can stop, start and run around obstacles easily.
Climbs stairs holding onto the railing (walks 2 feet to each step).
Pulls wheeled toy by string forward and backward.
Throws a small ball.
Walks into a large ball when intending to kick it.

Communication
Engages in simple pretend play.
Uses 50 or more recognizable words.
Puts together 2 or more words to formulate a sentence.
Asks "What's that?" constantly.
Joins in nursery rhymes and songs.
Refers to self by name.
Points to and repeats the names of body parts such as eyes, nose, hair, feet, mouth.
Understands simple commands and conversation.

Vision
Names familiar miniature toys at a distance of ten feet away.
Enjoys picture books, pointing to details on command.

Growing Child 36 MONTHS

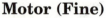

Developmental Check List

Social and Emotional
Eats with spoon and fork.
Washes hands but needs supervision for drying.
Dry during the day and often through the night.
Plays with other children in and outdoors.
Is affectionate toward younger children.
Likes to help adults with chores.
Pulls pants up and down but can't button yet.
Cooperates generally.
Shares toys.

Motor (Fine)
Builds a tower of 9 blocks.
Copies a bridge made with3 blocks.
Copies a circle with crayon on paper.
Draws figure of a man which appears as a head with 1 or 2 features.
Paints with large brush and paint.
Closes fist and wiggles thumb (right or left).

Motor (Gross)
Alternates feet when walking up stairs, (Comes down with
   2 feet to each step).
Rides tricycle.
Walks on tiptoes.
Stands on one foot momentarily when shown.
Jumps from bottom step of stairs.

Communication
Gives full name, sex, age when asked.
Asks questions "who?" "what?" "where?"
Enjoys listening to stories and wants favorite ones repeated
   over and over.
Recites nursery rhymes.
Uses plurals.
Uses large vocabulary but speech may contain misarticula-
   tions.
Engages in a simple conversation.
Talks about past experiences.
Uses pronouns "I, me, you" correctly.
Eager to talk about self and experiences with some stutter-
   ing not uncommon.

Vision
Matches 2 or3 primary colors (usually red and yellow).

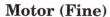

Growing Child 48 MONTHS

Developmental Check List

Social and Emotional

Eats well with fork and spoon.
Dresses and undresses self except for laces, back buttons and some snaps.
Prefers companionship of other children to adults.
Understands taking turns.

Motor (Fine)

Threads small beads if the needle is threaded first.
Builds a tower of 10 or more blocks.
Holds and uses a crayon or pencil with good control.
Copies an "O" (circle), "+" (plus), and "V."
Draws a house.

Motor (Gross)

Can bend and touch toes without bending knees.
Likes a variety of ball play.
Runs on toes.
Climbs, slides, swings actively.
Walks skillfully on narrow line or cracks in sidewalk.
Can stand on one foot (either foot) for 8 seconds.
Can hop forward (each foot) 2 yards.

Communication

Tells connected stories of recent experiences.
Can give name, address and age (may show on fingers).
Asks questions constantly – "why?" "what?" "how?" "when?"
Knows several nursery rhymes and can repeat or sing them correctly.
Counts by memory up to twenty.
Enjoys jokes.
Listens to and enjoys stories.
Speaks grammatically and exhibits only a few sounds substitutions (r-l-w-y group, p-th-f-s group or k-t group).

Growing Child 60 MONTHS

Developmental Check List

Social and Emotional
Dresses and undresses independently.
Uses knife and fork competently.
Washes and dries hands and face well.
Selects own playmates.
Is protective toward younger children and animals.
Comprehends rules of games and the concept of fair play.
Demonstrates a sense of humor.
Understands the necessity for tidiness, but requires frequent reminders.
Experiences fears involving self – dogs, falling, physical dangers.
Picks nose, bites nails.
Sucks thumb only before falling asleep or when fatigued.

Speech and Language
Speaks fluently except for a few mispronunciations (s, v, f, th).
Gives full name, age, birthday, address.
Defines concrete words by their function.
Asks meaning of abstract words and unfamiliar words and
    uses them subsequently.
Loves to recite and chant jingles and rhymes.
Enjoys being read to or told stories, and acts them out alone later.

Visual–Motor Skills
Threads a large needle independently and sews real stitches.
Copies circle, square, cross and capital letters VTHOXLYUCA.
Draws a house with these features: outline, door, windows,
    chimney, and roof.
Draws a person with these features: head, arms, legs, trunk.
Draws a variety of other items and names them *before* producing.
Uses brush, crayons and pencil with control.
Crayons and colors forms within the lines.
Matches 10 colors.
Names at least 4 primary colors.
Copies block patterns containing 10 blocks.

Motor Development
Can walk a narrow line without stepping off. Climbs, swings,
    runs skillfully. Moves rhythmically to music.
Stands on one foot (either foot) with arms folded across chest to
    a count of 10 seconds.
Hops 2-3 yards forward on each foot.
Enjoys ball play and understands rules, positions, and scoring.
Bends and touches toes without bending knees.
Grips strongly with each hand.
Can run lightly on toes.

Section 1—Color

Introduction

Color is everywhere and children respond to color very early. Learning the names for different colors should be part of a child's natural development.

Parents and teachers of very young children can aid this learning process by naming colors as they speak. For example, when a very young child points to an object and asks "What's that?" the response should include the color: "a red ball," "a blue flower," "a yellow bird," and so on. This should be done with all colors, even mixed or unusual colors such as turquoise, magenta, tan, rust, or any other colors you may find. By naming colors immediately and continuing to do so, the children will eventually relate the color words to the color itself.

It is important to begin reading to the children when they are very young. As you read or share picture books, discuss the pictures in terms of colors, shapes, sizes, and so on. You can choose a different focus each time if you like. On the first reading, for example, you could talk about all the colors which appear in the book. Another time, you might discuss the size or shape of the objects on each page.

Each reading, each emphasis will reinforce the concepts which the children need for learning readiness. At some point the children will begin to recognize colors, correctly finding or naming one or more colors in their games and activities. When you observe this, have them begin to play color games. Following are games and activities to help the children "learn" color.

This section presents activities from the very simple to the more complex. Two and three year old children should be able to grasp the simple lessons. The more complex activities can be done as they mature and become ready to start some type of schooling. They are not "graded" as such, but form a kind of natural progression.

Read through all of the activities and select those that you think suit your children or those that sound interesting.

These activities *do not* have to be taken in the order in which they appear. *They can and should be used with other activities found in the sections on shape, size, and direction.*

Art materials are very important especially when learning color. Have a good supply of art materials: crayons, chalk, paint, finger paint, colored paper, and drawing paper on hand. As soon as the children are ready to work with any art medium, with or without supervision, and can handle the materials responsibly, they should be coloring or painting and talking about color as they use and experiment with it. Help them to discover the joy of making their own colors by mixing finger paints, food coloring, play dough, and so on.

Take *frequent* field trips to a library, art museum, or gallery if you have them available. Even a short visit once a week will spur the children's interest and learning skills.

Activity 1

Color Recognition

When the children begin to recognize a color and repeat the name of the color, begin collecting objects of the same color. Example: If the children correctly name or find a blue ball, praise them. Then have them find other blue objects. Repeat the color word with the name of the object: blue glass, blue crayon, blue bird, blue paper, blue chair, and so on. After doing this several times, ask the children to search out objects of the color without your help. When they can do this, move on to another color that they recognize.

This type of activity should be done as a game, *informally*, and may be done over several days or even weeks. If the children tire, *stop the activity*.

Activity 2

Find the Color

When the children know two or more colors, gather several objects for each of these colors and a few objects of new colors. Place them on the table or floor. For example, you may have four blue objects, three red objects, four green objects, and one or two objects in colors which the children may not have practiced. Objects can be large or small: toys, stuffed animals, crayons, pencils, books, blocks, and so on. Ask the children to put together all of the blue objects, then all of the red objects, and so on until all objects are grouped by color. Help them count the number of objects in each group. Ask the children if they see any more things in the room which have the colors in the groups.

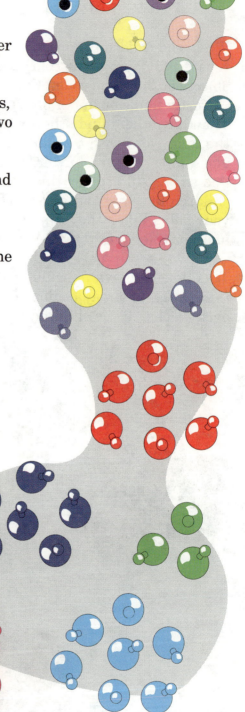

18

Find the Color

When the children can do *Activity Two* easily or begin to tire of it, reverse the process. Have the children send the parent or teacher on a search for colors that the children name. It may be good to pick one or two items which are variations of the color to show the children that there can be more than one shade of blue or red. It may also be good to include one or two items which are not the color chosen to see if the children recognize them.

Another activity would be to have the children gather their own selection of items to place on the table for another child or the parent to put into color groups. Items may include things made from colored paper by the children.

Activity 4

Color Collages

When children are able to select pictures and tear or cut paper (with or without help) have them begin making collages.

1. Have the children go through old magazines or catalogs and find pictures of things which are a certain color.

2. Cut the pictures out and glue them on a sheet of paper with the name of the color on the page.

3. These pages can be hung on the wall or bulletin board or made into a book (*Activity Seventeen*). Displaying the children's work and going back over it often is important for learning.

You may want to combine this activity with those in the size and shape sections.

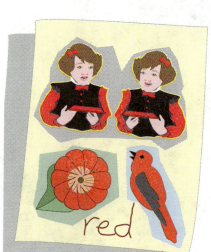

Activity 5

Color Mobiles

Make color mobiles:

1. Cut colorful pictures from magazines, cut simple shapes from colored paper, or have the children draw color pictures to be cut out.

2. Attach each to a string or thread and suspend it from a hanger or stick.

3. Be careful to balance the pictures so that the mobile does not tilt to one side.

4. Hang the mobile in the children's room.

5. Color names may be written on the simple objects, if desired.

6. Make a mobile for each new color learned.

Activity 6

Nature Walk

This activity and the following projects and activities can be continued as the children's awareness of color grows. Take a nature walk or visit a local botanical garden. Discuss all the colors and variations of color found in nature. Let the children find as many colors as they can. Document the experience in one or more of the following *Activities Seven* through *Twelve*.

Activity 7

Chart the Colors

Make a large chart of the colors in nature. Include the varying colors of such things as flowers, trees, animals, birds, rocks, sky, clouds, sunrises, sunsets, or the rainbow. Let the children help decide how to organize the chart. For example, do they want to organize it by color (putting all the natural things that contain red in one section); by types using headings such as colors of flowers, colors of rocks, and colors of birds; or can they think of another way to show the colors.

Color Chart
red
blue
yellow
green
orange
black
pink
gray
purple

or

Color Chart	
red	brown
blue	aqua
yellow	violet
green	pink
orange	gray
black	purple

or

Color Chart
Flowers
Rocks
Birds
Fruits
Leaves
Butterflies

  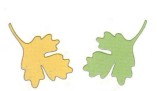

Activity 8

Make a Nature Book

Have the children begin a nature book. Add to the book as new discoveries are made. The book could be divided into sections. For example: Green Things in Nature, Red Things in Nature, The Many Colors of Leaves, The Many Colors of Flowers, The Many Colors of the Rainbow, Animals Come in Many Colors.

The type of division will depend on the age and the learning ability of the children. This activity could be repeated each year using a different focus.

Combine this book with concepts found in other sections. It could include a section on shapes in nature, size differences in nature, and so on. See related book activities in other sections.

The binding for this book could be a loose leaf binder. Make pages for the book of construction paper or heavy typing paper to fit the size of the binder. Punch holes in the paper or insert pages into plastic sleeves before putting them into the book.

For greater durability, laminate the pages with clear contact plastic. If such service is available, you could laminate the pages professionally.

Activity 9

Nature Collection

Collect leaves, flowers, seeds, feathers, colored rocks, or other easily collected natural objects.

Dry leaves or small flowers by pressing them in a book or under a heavy object or dry them in sand or borax. Hang bouquets of larger flowers or herbs to dry. Some of the dried flowers and leaves could be used to make natural arrangements for the table, for gifts, or to make special cards.

With the less fragile natural objects, set up a nature corner in an area where it can be seen, touched, and appreciated.

Discuss the colors and the variety of shapes and sizes that occur in nature. Combine this with activities in other sections. Add to and refer to the wonders of nature often. Children are very interested in the natural world and can learn a great deal from it.

Activity 10

Changing Color in Nature

1. Talk about the changing colors in nature. Have the children study a tree or bush which changes colors with the seasons. Have them collect leaves at each stage and in each season and point out the differences. Help the children to keep track of the changes either by drawing pictures of the different colored leaves, or by preserving the leaves and displaying them in a box, mounting on cardboard, or in a special book.

2. Talk about other natural things which change color. Watch a sunset together and talk about the colors. Compare them to the colors at sunrise and at midday. Have the children draw pictures or make a story about the different "colors" of the sun.

3. Observe the sky together on clear, breezy, cloudy, and stormy days. Ask the children to point out color differences caused by changes in the weather. Let them choose a way to record what they have seen.

4. Find books about color changes in nature, especially those which demonstrate how certain birds, animals, and reptiles can change their colors to provide protection. If possible, visit a pet store, zoo, or science museum which has a chameleon or other lizards which change colors. Have the children draw pictures of the animal in its various colors. Place it in the nature book or nature corner.

5. Have the children think about what it would be like if people could change color to hide themselves. Have them make up a story, illustrate it, and tell someone about it. Print the story for the children to keep.

Activity 11

Let's Draw Rainbows

Talk about the colors of the rainbow, how they are formed, and the order in which they appear: reds, oranges, yellows, greens, blues, and violets.

Find pictures of rainbows in books or magazines and name the colors.

Have the children paint or draw a rainbow.

Make rainbows of different sizes for a rainbow mobile or collage.

Activity 12

Rainbow Science

1. Purchase an inexpensive plastic or glass prism.

2. Show the children how to "create" a rainbow by holding the prism at an angle to the sunlight.

3. Have them find the rainbow on the ground, wall, or wherever it can be found.

4. Look at the colors and the order of the colors.

5. Hang a prism or small reflector in a sunny window so that the children may see rainbows and reflections each day.

Color Games

Color games present a more formal, structured approach to learning. Children like to play more games as they grow older. The following games will help the children to organize their knowledge and will check the knowledge of the ten colors needed for kindergarten: red, blue, yellow, green, orange, purple, brown, pink, black, and white. Many games may be purchased which check both color and shape recognition. The following activities are simple games that can be made.

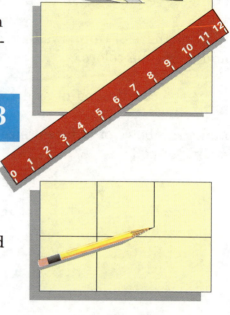

Activity 13

Lotto or Bingo

To make the game:

1. Begin with blank tagboard or white cardboard and cut four or five 5" x 8" cards. If you have only one child, make at least four cards using different combinations of colors and shapes.

2. Divide each card into six equal boxes.

3. Draw one basic shape in each box.

4. Color the shapes with markers.

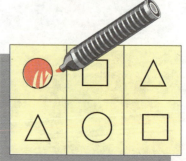

5. Cover each board with clear contact paper for longer wear.

6. When the boards are completed, make a set of individual answer cards to match each game card. For example, the sample card would require six answer cards.
   one red circle
   one blue square
   one yellow triangle
   one green triangle
   one black circle
   one orange square

When not in use, the answer cards can be kept in an envelope on the back of each game card.

To play the game:

This game can be played in a variety of ways.

1. A child picks an answer card from the envelope
    and places it on the matching square of the
    game card. This can be done independently or
    with help. This task is repeated until all of the
    squares are correctly matched. Once the child
    is familiar with the game, find another child or
    adult who will play a card at the same time as
    the child. See who can finish first!

2. The parent or another child can act as a caller.
    Answer cards are placed face down. The caller
    picks an answer card and calls out the color
    (and shape) on the card. The child must point
    to the correct space before placing it on the
    game card. Set a specific goal for the child:
    cover four corners, fill the whole card, or fill
    three squares across. When the goal is reached,
    the child "wins" the game.

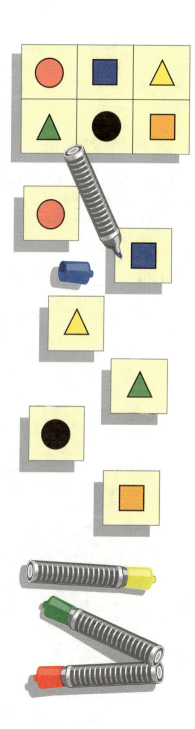

Activity 14

Memory

Many memory games are on the market. If you can find one for color (shape) matching, you may want to purchase it. If not, you can easily make one.

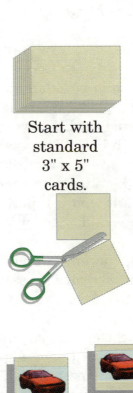

Start with standard 3" x 5" cards.

To make the game:

1. Take blank 3" x 5" cards and cut them in half giving you two cards 3" x 2 ½" inches each (twenty-two or twenty-six should be enough).

2. Make pairs of cards for the different colors. This can be done in several ways.

   a. Cut out matching colored pictures from a catalog or magazine (for example: two blue balloons, two red shoes, two green balls). Glue one picture on each card to make a pair of cards.

   b. Draw matching pictures on the cards.

   c. Draw matching colored shapes onto the cards to extend the use of the game into the next section. A memory set of twenty-six cards *may have* the following pairs:

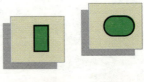

   red circles
   blue squares
   green triangles
   yellow ovals
   purple rectangles
   pink stars
   orange diamonds
   brown squares
   black triangles
   red octagons
   blue ovals
   green rectangles
   yellow stars

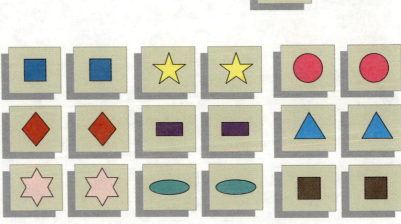

30

To play the game;

1. Place all of the cards *face down* on the table.

2. Separate the pairs (do not put the same two shapes next to each other).

3. The first player turns over any two cards.

4. If the cards match, the player may keep the pair and take another turn.

5. If the cards do not match, they are returned *face down* in the same position as before.

6. The next player then takes a turn.

7. The object of the game is to remember where the cards are placed on the table so that a pair can be made from a new card and one remembered from a previous turn.

8. The winner of the game is the one with the most pairs.

Note: If thirteen pairs (twenty-six cards) are too difficult for the children at first, cut the number of pairs to seven or nine until they understand the game. Gradually add more pairs as the children's skill level increases. This game should be fun as well as a learning activity. It should not frustrate the children. Adjust play according to their needs.

This game may also serve as a good matching activity for younger children. Mix the cards. Lay them *face up* on the table. Have the children find the matching cards. For example, two red circles.

31

Activity 15

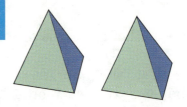

Color Sorting Games

Have the children make up sorting games by color using any materials available.

This could include sorting out the people in the room or house by their color of hair, eyes, or clothing.

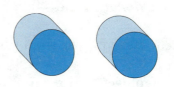

Children could also sort the button box, the material scraps, the flowers in the garden, or whatever they choose to sort by color.

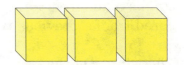

When doing this activity, see if the children can find other sorting categories such as shapes and sizes. This will prepare them for other sections or may be combined with other sections.

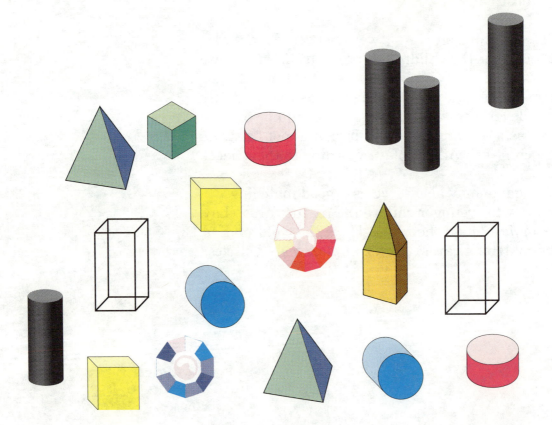

Activity 16

Pegboard Games

Use a large pegboard with multicolored pegs to play color sorting games.

Have the children line up all of the blue pegs in a row, followed by the red, green, orange, and so forth.

They could create color designs using the different colored pegs.

Let them make up a color game with the pegs.

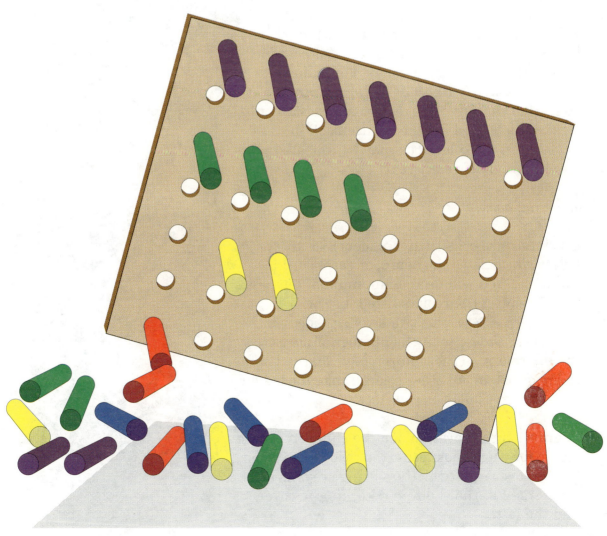

Activity 17

The "Big Book of Colors"

Children love to make big books. Begin the book when the children show an interest in putting a word or name together with an object. They do not need to be "reading" yet but may simply be asking questions about reading and words.

Tell the children that just as they have a name (print each child's name on paper or on a chalk board and let them trace it), so everything else in creation has a name—including colors. Explain that in your book you will put the name of each color on the top of a page in the book.

Show the children some books from the library or home. Help them to find the title of the book. Explain that "title" is another word for the "name" of the book. Ask the children to think of possible names for their book about colors. For example: *My Color Book*; *My Book of Colors*; *Colors, Colors, Everywhere*. Be creative and let the children take the lead. Like the nature book in *Activity Eight*, the color book may be repeated with a different emphasis each year.

To make the book:

1. Use large size construction paper (9" x 18") or larger white paper, tagboard, or cardboard if available. You will need a minimum of ten pages (one for each of the colors listed just prior to *Activity Thirteen*), plus two heavier sheets for the cover. *Do not* limit the number of pages to the ten colors. If the children have learned other colors or ask about other colors, make a page for each of these colors as well.

2. Begin with the cover. When the children choose a title for their book, print the title of the book on the cover in large letters using crayons or markers. Let the children decorate the cover and the letters.

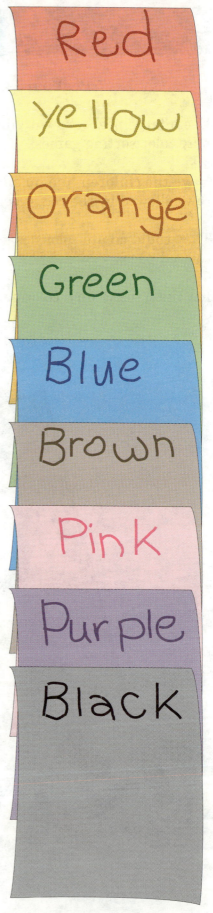

3. Show them that most books have an author. Have them print or trace their name on the cover of the Big Book.

4. Do one page of the book at a time. Let the children choose the color for the first page. Print the name of the color using a marker or crayon of the same color. For example, tell the children that the letters r-e-d spell the name of the color red. Write the word "red" in red marker or crayon at the top of the page and have the children paint or draw a patch of red color next to the word.

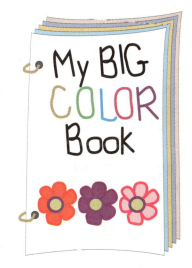

5. Then have the children find pictures in magazines or catalogs of red objects. They may also draw pictures of red objects, cut them out of red construction paper, or make designs with them (yarn, buttons, or any other suitable red objects).

6. Finally, have the children practice tracing or writing the word "red" with a red crayon, a pencil, or a marker.

7. Continue this activity throughout the year adding a new color when the children master it or are ready to move on to another color. After they have learned a color, review it often.

In a classroom, the teacher may want to extend the big book activity by having the children make their own color book in centers or as a parent-assisted home activity.

8. You may wish to make a folded book:

   a. Take several sheets of paper large enough to give a good-sized page when folded in half.

   b. Take heavier paper or tagboard for the cover and cut it so that it is one to one and a half inches larger than the paper on all sides.

   c. Fold the pages and the cover in half CARE-FULLY.

   d. Stitch the middle with a heavy needle and strong thread. (Heavy staples may be used.)

Activity 18

Using the Big Book Color Book

1. Have the children make up color stories about each color using the objects on the pages in the book made in *Activity Seventeen*.

2. Copy the stories down and attach them to the color page to be enjoyed again.

3. When doing the color book, have a painting day for each color. For example, have a painting day for red. Have red finger paint, watercolor, tempera, or paint sticks available as well as large sheets of paper. The children could use any or all of these to create their "red" picture. Hang up the picture or add it to the book.

"Yellow" Story

Duckie and his friend Chicken lived on a farm. They played in the yellow flowers every day. One day chicken said to Duckie, "Let's go over to the big yellow house on the corner and see if Mrs. Farmer has any yellow corn for us"

36

Activity 19

Color Pattern Games

1. Using any of the color sorting materials (blocks, cubes, bears, straws, buttons), lay out a simple pattern for the children to copy. See if they can copy the pattern using the same or other materials. Lay out three red blocks and one blue block followed by three more red and one blue. See if the children can then lay out the pattern of three red, and one blue. Vary the patterns: two red, two blue; three blue, one red; one blue, three red; and so forth. Have the children copy each pattern.

2. Vary the colors as well as the patterns, using only two colors at a time until the children have mastered the concept.

3. Have them make color patterns for you to copy.

4. When the children become proficient at two color patterns, move on to three color patterns.

5. Use the pegboard and colored pegs for pattern games. Set a pattern of pegs in one row and have the children copy it in the next row. When they can do this easily, have them set patterns for the parent or another child to copy.

6. Patterns may also be made with colored paper shapes glued on cards for the children to copy.

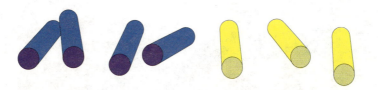

Activity 20

Color Pinwheels

1. Cut a circle of paper about six inches in diameter.

2. Divide it into six equal sections as is done in the illustration on this page.

3. Color the sections with a marker.

4. Make a hole in the center with a sharp pencil.

5. Insert the pencil through the hole (point down).

6. Spin the color wheel like a top.

7. Have the children describe what happens to all the colors.

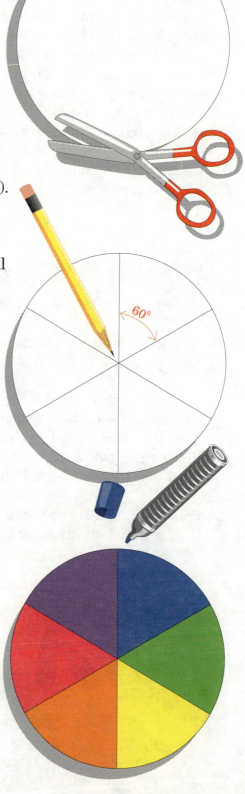

Activity 21

Color Mixing

Children are fascinated by color and the variety of colors everywhere. Provide an area and an opportunity for experimenting with color mixing. This can be done with food coloring, paints, finger paints, play dough, or other media which will allow colors to mix together to make new colors. This can be incorporated with lessons in the Big Color Book in *Activity Seventeen*.

When introducing the color green, experiment with mixing yellow and blue paints, yellow and blue food coloring, or yellow and blue play dough. Ask the children if they know any other names for the colors created (aqua, turquoise, chartreuse). The same type of activity can be done for orange (red-yellow), purple (blue-red), pink (white-red), gray (black-white), or brown (red and green or yellow and blue and red). See what other combinations the children can create.

Activity 22

Cooking with Colors

Children love to help in the kitchen. When working with color, do some "color cooking" with them. When studying red, for example, spend some time in the kitchen with at least one of the following.

1. Make some red gelatin, fruit punch, or popsicles.

2. Bake some sugar cookies and frost or decorate with red sugar or hearts.

3. Use some cookie dough to form the letters r-e-d and decorate with red.

4. Color some eggs.

5. Make a dish using red vegetables.

6. Make a cake and use food coloring in the frosting.

7. Adapt other cooking activities to holidays and seasonal colors.

Use similar activities for each color. When appropriate, make some natural dyes from berries and vegetables (purple cabbage, beets, and so forth). Use these natural dyes to color white yarn, or small pieces of cloth. Talk about the colors that people used from the plants they found around them. Find a book on the dyes used by the American Indians to make rugs and clothes.

Activity 23

Seasonal Colors

The different seasons of the year provide many opportunities for talking about specific colors.

Fall: Look at the color of leaves and Thanksgiving such as orange, brown, yellow, black, and gold. Talk about these colors and why they are used in the fall. Do art projects with fall or holiday themes which use these colors.

Christmas: Colors of Christmas trees, bows, ornaments, and decorations: red, green, silver, gold, and "sparkling" colors. Use holiday projects to reinforce these colors.

Winter: Blue, white, and grey are colors that are cool or cold. Snowflakes and snowman art projects still delight children even in climates where it does not snow. The holidays in this season have their own special colors like red for Valentine's Day.

Spring or Easter: The spring season reminds us of new budding life and colors like greens, yellow, pink, lavender, and the soft pastel hues. Look at the plants that bloom in the spring. Talk about the new life and the colors of the clothing people choose for their Easter outfit. Plan art projects which will incorporate the different colors of the season.

Summer: Patriotic colors, fireworks colors, and garden produce remind us of warm colors like red, white, blue, green and yellow. Reinforce the colors with projects that reflect the season.

Extended Activities

Do not overlook the opportunities for learning in the world around you. Have your children play color games while on walks, on field trips, driving in the car, or shopping in the grocery store or mall.

Children can learn a great deal traveling from one place to another. Use the travel time as learning time by creating games for your children. Have them search for different objects. For example, four red things, five blue things, or four green things, etc.

Have the children create their own games.

As the children progress, have them look for color words or for a certain number of shapes the same color. For example, stop signs, bus stop signs, and other common everyday objects.

As always, you are limited only by your surroundings and your imagination.

Section 2—Shapes

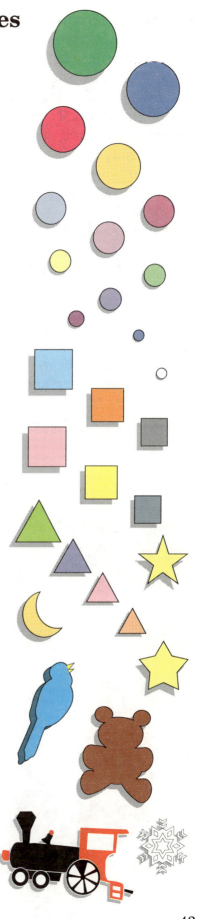

Introduction

Just as everything in the children's world has a color, so everything also has a shape. If school age children or adults were shown silhouettes of a bird, a plane, a car, or a person, they would have very little difficulty identifying the object by its shape.

Certain shapes, however, occur regularly both in the natural and the manufactured world. Very young children who play on the kitchen floor may begin their early experiences surrounded by squares, circles, octagons, triangles, or other common shapes found in floor tiles or carpeting. Their first toys may be pots, lids, baking pans, plastic containers, or wooden spoons—all of which contain common shapes (circles, ovals, etc.).

The experience of shape begins as early as the experience of color. Using the correct terms early and consistently helps children to form a framework for the later understanding of shapes. For example, answer their "What's that?" question with phrases like, "a round ball," "a round red ball," "a circle," or "a square pan," when appropriate. The circle in the picture may be a ball, a sun, or a moon. Make the connection between the object and its shape, for example "That's the sun. It looks like a circle."

Using shape names, with very young children, does not come as naturally as using color names. As the children get older and begin to ask more questions about the properties of the objects they see or about the pictures they see in books, these terms can be used more effectively.

Games and activities to help the children learn shapes will follow many of the same guidelines as those games and activities used to help them learn color. The following suggested games and activities will give the parent or teacher some ideas for learning shapes. They are presented with easier activities first and progress to the more difficult. Read through all of the activities and games before you begin and select those which will benefit your children most.

The earlier activities are not formal lessons. You do not need to go straight through. They may be used along with or as alternatives to similar activities in other sections which match your children's abilities.

As in all areas, reinforce all concepts by reading to your children or by making frequent trips to libraries, museums, and other resources in your area.

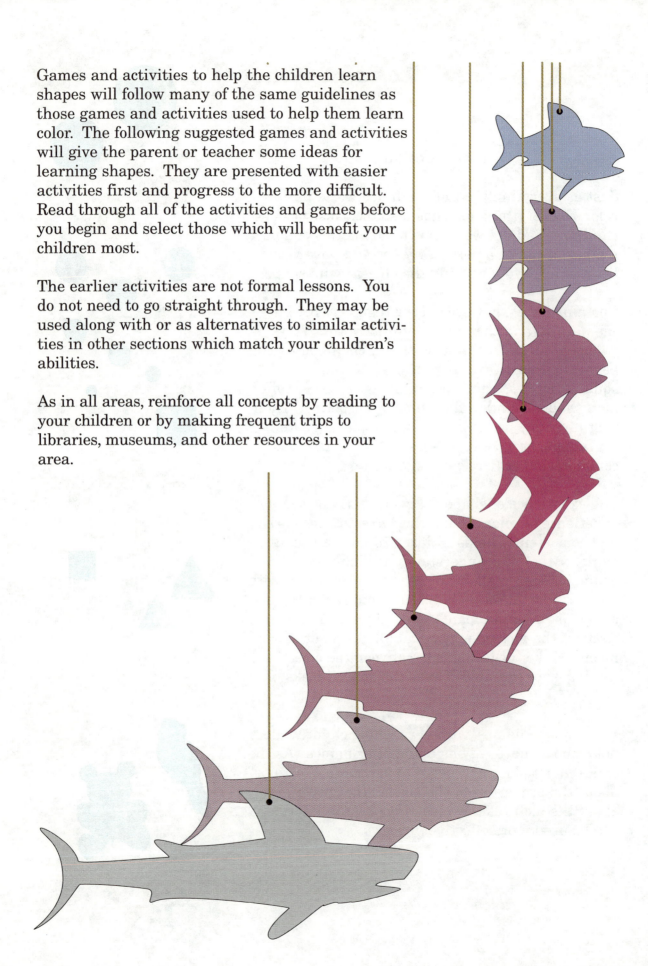

Activity 1

Basic Shapes

Cut several sets of basic shapes (circle, square, triangle, rectangle, oval, octagon, star, diamond, and heart) from various materials like cardboard or colored tagboard. Use these shapes for tracing and comparing with objects around the house or classroom. To add another dimension to these projects cut the shapes out of materials that allow the children to feel textural differences. Use felt shapes on a felt board; rug pieces, foam rubber, sponges, or styrofoam in art projects; or sandpaper for paper rubbings.

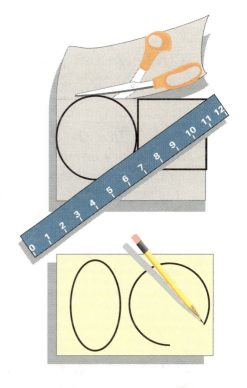

These shapes can be used for preschool through grade school activities. Use some or all of the materials above or choose some you think are appropriate. Cardboard or tagboard shapes will last longer if they are covered with clear contact paper.

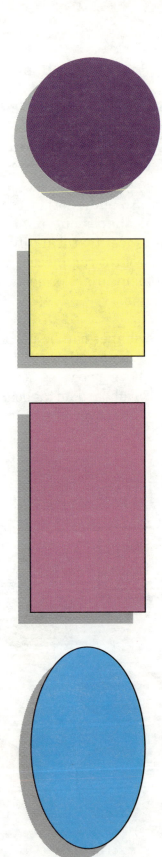

Activity 2

Recognizing the Shapes

1. **Circle:** As the children are learning to recognize a shape, help them to understand the properties of the shape. Draw a circle on a sheet of paper and tell the children the name of the shape. Have the children trace the circle with their finger or a crayon and say the name with you. If the children are interested in words at this stage, write out the word "circle" and have the children trace the letters and say the word. Point out to the children that a circle is a "smooth" shape. It has no corners. Continue to work on the circle as long as it holds the children's interest or until it has been mastered. If they tire of the activity, stop and return to it later.

2. **Square:** As the children become familiar with squares, point out or let them discover the differences between circles and squares. Have the children feel the corners of the square pattern or of a square object. Is it smooth like a circle? Discover other differences. Does a square completely cover a circle of the same size? Does a circle cover a square of the same size? Why?

3. **Rectangle:** Introduce the rectangle as a "stretched square." Demonstrate that a rectangle also has corners like a square. Use square boxes and rectangular boxes to help demonstrate the differences. Have the children search for square and rectangular windows, blocks, building blocks, books and baking pans.

4. **Oval:** Introducing the oval as a "stretched circle" will help the children make the association. Note that the oval, like the circle, has no corners. It is smooth. Help them to find ovals around the house and the yard. Look for oval windows, oval picture frames, and so forth. When you cook, allow the children to discover that an egg is an oval.

5. **Triangle:** Have the children point out the differences between the triangle and the other shapes they have learned (three sides, sharper corners, etc.). Ask them if it is possible to balance an object on the tip of a triangle.

6. **Octagon:** The children can learn about the shape of an octagon more quickly once they begin to associate the shape with the familiar *stop* sign. Help them to note differences (eight sides, corners not as sharp). If you have pattern blocks available, help the children to see how other shapes can fit around an octagon.

7. **Star**, **heart**, **and diamond:** These are common shapes that the children will encounter throughout life. These shapes appear in books. They are common shapes for rewards and stickers for charts. They are also shapes that most children enjoy learning to draw. These initial shape activities are to be done at the children's pace. They are games rather than "formal" lessons. If something becomes tiring, leave it for a while (a few days or even weeks) then try again until the understanding is there. Add variety to the activities by combining them with activities in the color and size sections.

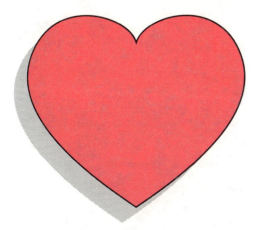

Activity 3

Shape Pictures

As the children are able, have them trace the cardboard shapes and cut them out. They may want to trace the shapes on plain paper and color them, to trace them on colored paper or wallpaper samples, or to trace several shapes in different sizes. They can then decorate the shapes, or use them to make shape pictures.

Activity 4

Shape Prints

Using the sponge or foam shapes the children cut out in *Activity One*, let them make shape prints. Dip the sponge or foam into a small amount of paint and print on plain paper. You may also do this by brushing a small amount of paint onto the styrofoam or rug shapes before you print. Try different colors, overlapping shapes, and shape animals or scenes.

Shape prints can also be carved out of potatoes and used to make prints.

Mixed Media Shaped Pictures

Have the children make shape pictures using a variety of media: fingerpaint, clay, chalk, crayon, marker, poster paints, and pipe cleaners. Ask them to paint or to draw a large circle, square, or triangle on the paper. Have the children make a picture using that shape. They may use any of the materials to do this. For example, the children may turn the circle into a sun, a ball, the wheels of a cart, a lollipop, the head of a person or animal, a moon, or some other object they perceive as circular. If they cannot think of anything to do with their shape, make some suggestions to help make the connection.

This activity helps the parent or teacher evaluate the children's ability to associate the abstract shape with the objects in their world. If they have difficulties continue to review previous activities.

Activity 6

Shape Collages

Have the children look through magazines and catalogs with you to find pictures of things with various shapes. Make a collage for each individual shape, for two or more shapes, or for mixed shapes as they are learned.

Making the collage:

1. When you have found pictures of things for your collage, search around for other materials which can be added: buttons, felt shapes, bottle caps, pipe cleaners formed into shapes, pieces of wrapping paper or cellophane, material scraps, contact paper.

2. After you and your children have gathered all these materials, take a large sheet of paper or tagboard and let the children arrange the materials on the sheet to fill the entire paper.

3. Help them to glue the objects down. Don't worry if they overlap.

4. When the collage is finished, ask the children to give it a title. With a marker, print the title on the collage. Letters may run over the top of objects and pictures.

5. Hang the collage in a place where it can be seen by the whole family.

6. Have the children make up stories about the things in the collage. See if they can create a story about the shape(s) in the collage. Write the story and attach it to the collage.

Activity 7

Shape Mobile

The shape mobile can be made in several ways depending on the materials used. Mobiles may represent a single shape or several shapes at once.

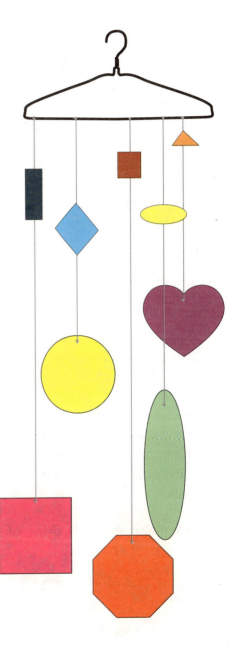

1. Have the children find or make pictures of objects which represent the shape or shapes to be used in the mobile.

2. Choose materials which can be balanced with the other materials used.

3. Find two or three sticks and bind them together in the middle or find a metal coat hanger from which to hang the shapes (see illustration).

4. Use bright colored string, yarn, or ribbon to hang each shape.

5. Other ideas include:

   a. Make shapes from colored paper and hang them. Use contrasting colors and varying sizes.

   b. Cut pictures from magazines or catalogs, mount them on colored paper, and hang them.

   c. Make shapes or objects which contain the shapes from flexible materials such as pipe cleaners. Suspend them on a string from sticks or a hanger.

   d. Cut shapes out of foil or shiny wrapping paper.

   e. Let your children select objects for different shapes which are not too heavy to hang.

   f. Let the children suggest other possibilities or use a combination of the suggestions listed to create the mobile.

Hang the finished mobile where the children can watch it.

Activity 8

Shapes in Nature

This activity may be done in addition to or separate from the colors in nature projects found in the *Color Section Activities Six* through *Twelve*. The children may want to collect some natural shapes. For example, round or oval seeds and round or oval flowers or flower petals. These can be added to a nature book or used to begin a new book. They may also be collected and placed in the nature corner.

Do not limit this activity to basic shapes. Have the children collect "nature shapes" such as different shaped leaves, flowers, and rocks.

This is a good time to discuss the fact that all things have a shape. Have the children talk about how these nature shapes are alike and how they are different. Point out that certain groups of items can have different shapes and still belong to the same group. Leaves, for example, come in many shapes, but we still recognize them as leaves. The same can be said for flowers and rocks.

Have the children think of some other natural groups of shapes.

Activity 9

Shape Pattern Games

Shape pattern cards and blocks are readily available. They can also be easily made.

1. Begin with a simple pattern using pattern blocks or pattern shapes cut from heavy construction paper. Set a pattern for the children. For example: circle, triangle, square or triangle, square, circle. Have the children repeat the pattern with their own shape blocks. Vary the shape patterns once the children catch on to the game. Do not rush them. If they tire or find this activity too difficult, pick another activity and return to this one later.

2. As the children progress, add more shapes or add a color pattern to the shape pattern. For example, two red triangles, one blue circle, and three green squares. Have them repeat the pattern.

3. Make sets of pattern cards for the children to use independently when they are familiar with the patterning activities.

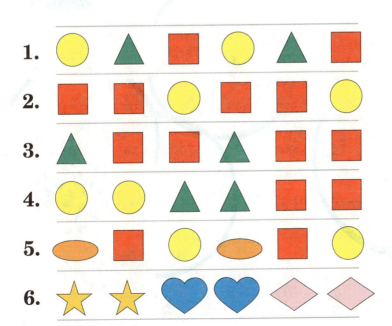

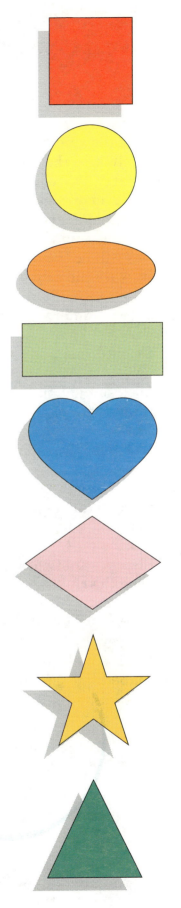

53

Activity 10

Shape Hunt

Have the children start on a "circle hunt" and find all the things in the room that have a circle in them. To help the children you may want to let them carry a cardboard circle shape with them as they look for circles in the room. Progress through the different shapes the children have learned on succeeding hunts. Some of the more difficult shapes will not be mastered until the children are older. Vary the activity from day to day.

1. Select a different room.

2. Go outdoors.

3. Look through magazines and catalogs to find things with circles.

4. Watch for circles in stores, in church, and on signs.

5. Look for circles along the way while riding in the car.

6. Place a variety of shape cards on the table and have the children find the circles.

7. Place a variety of objects on the table (pennies, straws, buttons, checkers, pencils) and ask the children to pick out the objects shaped like circles.

When the children are able, let them direct the hunt and send the parent searching for a specific shape. When selecting shapes, include one or two which are *not* the shape requested. This is not done to confuse the children, but will help you to see if the children can distinguish the shapes.

If you are working on other sections at the same time, incorporate the concepts. For example, if you have been working on the color hunt activity and introducing basic shapes, have the children search for things by shape and color. Find round red objects, find all the blue square blocks, and so on.

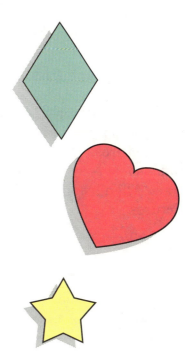

Activity 11

Shape Picture Activity

1. When the children are ready, move from pattern cards, which are merely lines of shapes, to pattern pictures. On paper or at the chalk board, make some easy pattern pictures for the children. Then let the children make some pattern pictures.

2. As the children get used to pattern pictures, find more difficult examples which do not have the shapes clearly outlined. See if the children can decide which shapes make up the picture.

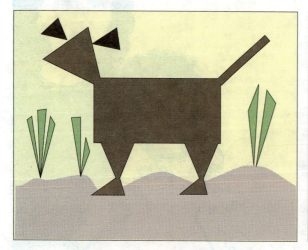 

Activity 12

Shape Games

Shape games can be purchased or made. Games such as lotto, bingo, and memory can reinforce the shapes that have been learned. Directions for making these games can be found in the *Color Section Activity Thirteen* and *Fourteen*.

To make the games a little more difficult, use pictures of objects which are the same but have different shapes (leaves, trees, cars, etc.) instead of the simple shapes given in the directions.

Activity 13

Shape Puzzles

To make shape puzzles, take a large picture from an old calendar. Glue it to cardboard. Cut simple shapes according to the children's abilities. For longer durability, cover each piece with clear contact paper. Keep the puzzles in large envelopes and mark a code on the back to aid sorting later.

For children who are more advanced, try some simple tangram puzzles. A tangram is a Chinese puzzle consisting of a square cut into five triangles, a square, and a rhomboid, to be reassembled into different figures. Tangram books and puzzles can be purchased or made. A pattern for tangram shapes follows as well as some easy tangram design pictures to use with the children. Encourage them to make their own tangram shape pictures.

Tangram Shapes: Cut out of heavy construction paper or cardboard.

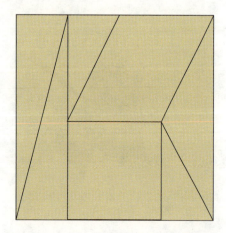
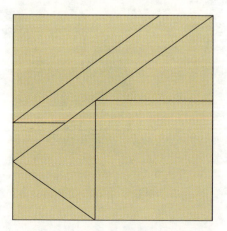

58

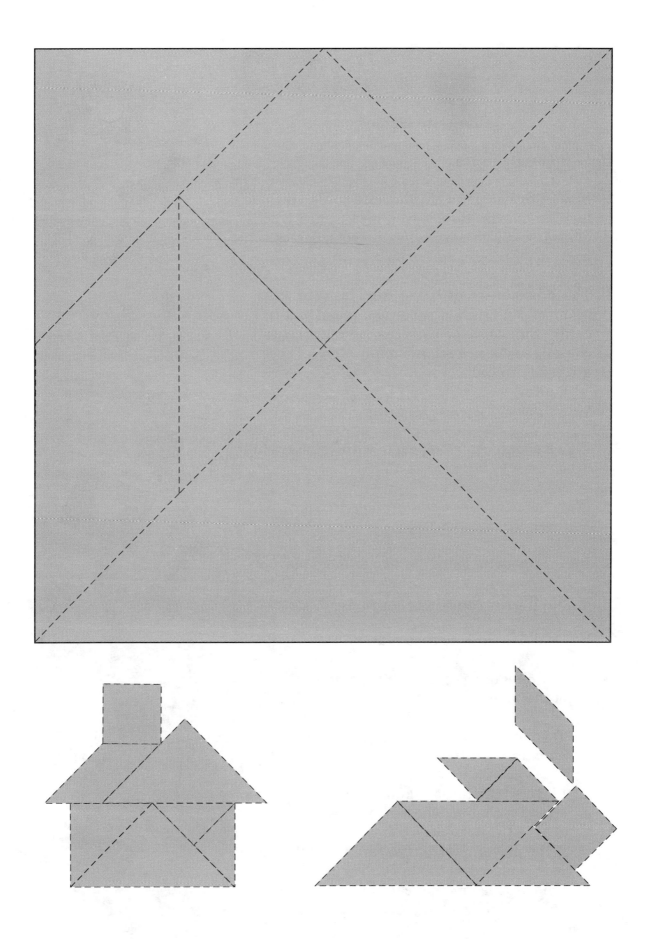

Activity 14

Silhouette Games

Make silhouette games:

1. Make thirteen pairs of silhouette cards. Include familiar things: cars, leaves, birds, trees, trucks, planes, stop signs, stars, hearts, pots, horses, cows, dogs, people, and so on.

2. The silhouettes may be cut from black or other colors of construction paper and glued to 3" x 5" cards. Simple shape patterns can often be purchased in sets at a school supply store. These are easily traced.

Playing silhouette games:

1. Play a simple matching game with younger children.

2. Play "memory" (see *Color Section Activity Fourteen* for directions).

3. Play "Silhouette Pairs" for two or more players:

   a. Shuffle the cards.

   b. Deal five cards to each player.

   c. Put remaining cards face down in the center of the table.

   d. Take any pairs dealt to the player out of the hand and put them face down on the table.

   e. Players take turns asking other players for a silhouette that matches one in their hand.

   f. If the player receives the card requested, the pair is placed on the table. The player may then request another card.

g. If the player does not receive the card, a card is drawn from the central pack.

h. If the card requested is drawn, the player may continue to ask.

i. If the player does not draw the matching card, the next player takes a turn.

j. Play continues until all pairs are matched.

k. The player with the most pairs is the winner.

4. Play "Old Silhouette" (just like "Old Maid"):

a. Remove one silhouette from the deck. Show everyone which one has been removed.

b. Deal all of the cards. Choose a number of pairs and cards that little hands can manage.

c. Players take turns picking a card from another player's hand. If two are playing, they pick from each other. If three or more are playing, each person picks from the person on his left.

d. Pairs are put aside on a pile next to each player.

e. The player who is left with the single unpaired silhouette is "Old Silhouette" or loser.

Activity 15

Shape Containers

If possible, select containers for shapes which correspond to the shape:

1. A large round container for circular objects.

2. A large square box for square objects; a large rectangular box for rectangular objects.

3. A large square or rectangular box which can be divided *diagonally* to form two triangular sections for triangular objects.

Let the children decorate the containers with drawings or pictures cut from magazines or catalogs to illustrate the shape.

Use a marker to print the name of the shape on the box or container.

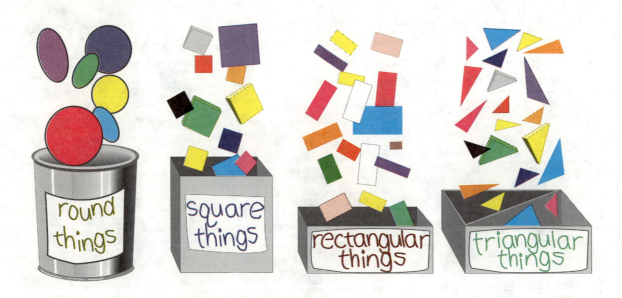

Activity 16

Shape Collections

Have the children collect objects, pictures of objects, or drawings of objects and place them in the correct boxes. This collection can be added to or changed at any time. Use these collected objects in a variety of ways.

1. Sort objects of the same shape into different groups (color or size).

2. Have the children reach into the box without looking and describe what they feel. The parent or other children can try to guess what the object is. This is a good activity for identifying objects by touch.

3. Make up stories or pictures about a particular shape or all the different objects which have that shape.

4. Talk about the similarities and differences between objects of the same shape.

5. Let the children make up their own games and activities with the objects in each box.

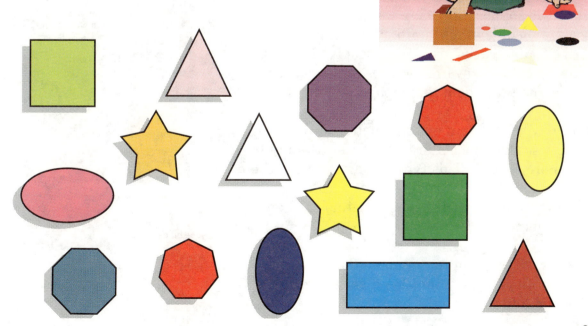

Activity 17

Shape Inventory Charts

Using a large tagboard, make a shapes inventory chart or charts for the individual shapes.

This can be done in several ways (see examples).

Have the children draw or cut and paste pictures of objects from each room for the shapes listed. This activity can be expanded by making additional charts for things seen in the park, in the grocery store, in the mall, in church, or along the road as seen from the car.

Activity 18

Big Book of Shapes

Make a big book of shapes (see *Color Section Activity Seventeen* for general directions and use). Do not limit the children to basic shapes.

When the children have completed the pages for the basic shapes, they may want to expand the book to include other familiar shapes such as cars, birds, boats, trucks, trees, and people. Have them draw or cut out several pictures of the chosen shape and glue them to the page.

You may want to cut out silhouettes of these objects so that the children may see the similarities more clearly. This type of activity gives them good practice in recognizing categories as well as helping to talk about objects in terms of likenesses and differences.

Encourage the children to make up stories for some or all of the pages in the shape book. Print the stories and add them to the book.

SHAPES IN MY HOME

	●	◻	△	▭
Kitchen				
Living Room				
Bedroom				

Circles Around Me

Shapes By Room: KITCHEN

Bind your book together with string or yarn,

OR

. . .try making holes with a standard punch and using brass fasteners,

OR

. . .punch pages at the top and use binder rings.

The shape of the book itself can be very creative. Choose the shape of the book according to the subject matter. For a book on leaves, find or make a large pattern of a leaf. Trace this pattern on construction paper for the cover of the book. Trace the same pattern on as many sheets of plain paper as needed. The same principle can be applied to books on fish, cars, shapes, and any other subject that can be made from a simple outline pattern.

Activity 19

Letter and Number Shapes

When the children are ready, begin a simple discussion of number and letter shapes.

1. Form letter and number shapes on a board or paper with clay, play dough, pattern blocks or whatever is available.

2. Talk about the shapes or parts of shapes that can be seen in many letters and numbers. For example: circles, triangles, squares, lines, corners, and ovals.

3. Make a number or letter shape poster and divide it by individual shapes. For example, all numbers or letters that contain circles.

Have the children trace those number or letter shapes which they recognize.

Activity 20

Geoboard Shapes
(Pegboards and pegs may also be used.)

Make or purchase two geoboards. Using one geoboard, make a shape pattern. Have the children copy the pattern on to the second geoboard. Begin with a simple pattern of one shape and move on to more complex patterns using two or more shapes as the children's skills grow.

A simple pattern would be a circle, a triangle, or other easily recognized shapes. These simple patterns may also include numbers and letters if the children are familiar with them.

A more complex pattern would include shape pictures such as a house formed from a triangle for the roof, a square or rectangle for the main part of the house, a smaller square or squares for windows, and a smaller rectangle for a door. Complex patterns may also include a shape inside another shape, such as a triangle inside a square.

When the children can copy the patterns with minimum difficulty, have them make patterns for a parent or other children to copy. Have the children copy favorite patterns on geopaper and save to use as patterns for another time. Patterns for making a geoboard and for geopaper can be found on the following pages.

Simple Shapes:

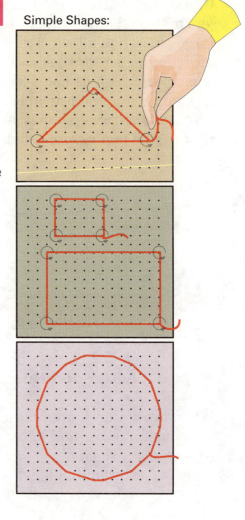

Complex Shapes:

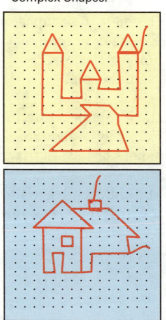

Making a Geoboard

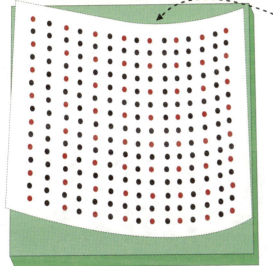

1. Buy or cut a piece of board ½" to ¾" thick and measuring 8" x 8". A piece of 1" x 8" plank is suitable, as is ½" or ¾" plywood. It is easier on little hands if the wood is sanded smooth on the edges and corners. You may want to paint or varnish your board at this time.

2. Cut out the easy-to-use template on the next page and mark where each nail "peg" should be driven by piercing each dot with a push-pin or tack while the template is in place over your board. You should fasten the template to the board with tape to keep things lined up and steady.

3. Drive headless nails such as 4d (called "four penny") or 6d (called "six penny") finishing nails into your board in the marks you made with the template. Be especially careful to drive each nail to the same depth in the wood. *For a simpler board, use only the red dots.*

   You may also wish to file any sharp burs off the heads of the nails.

   Your geoboard is now ready to use!

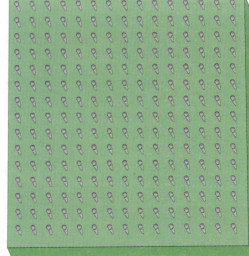

Geoboard Template

You will want to use this template to help make your geoboard project easier. For a simpler board, use every other dot (the red dots). For a more versatile board, use all the dots. YOU MAY REPRODUCE THIS PAGE as often as you like for use with your children on this project.

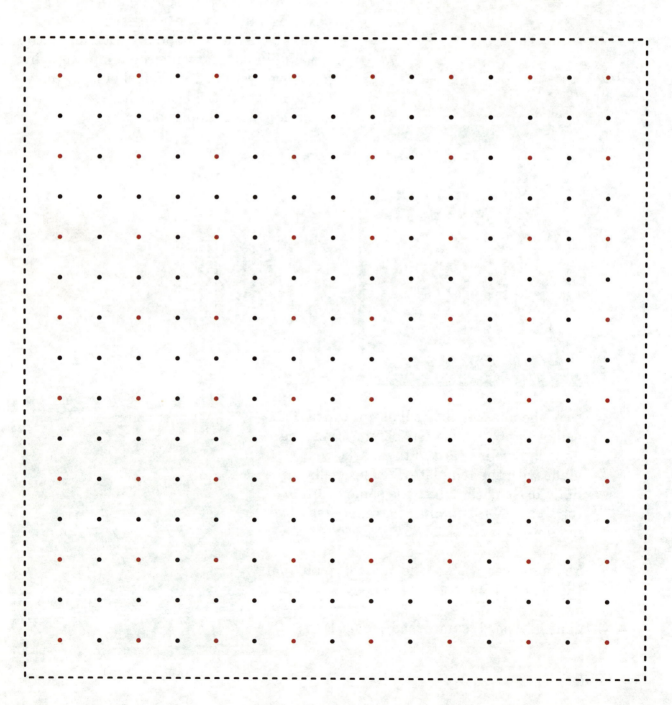

Activity 21

Cooking with Shapes

Extend the shape activities to the kitchen by using some of the following suggestions or your own ideas.

1. Bake shape cookies or biscuits (a sugar cookie recipe or a baking powder biscuit dough will work).

   a. Begin with the basic shapes. Advance to other shapes such as dinosaurs or other animals.

   b. Holiday shapes such as pumpkins, bells, Christmas trees, stars, gingerbread men, angels, and hearts can be used.

   c. Make the shapes by drawing your own or using cookie cutters.

This could be a "treat" after several shapes are learned. This activity may also be combined with *Activity Twenty-Two* in the *Color Section*.

2. To make "Knox Blocks" use four envelopes of unflavored gelatin and four cups of fruit juice: two cups of cold fruit juice with gelatin sprinkled on top and two cups of boiling fruit juice stirred until the gelatin is dissolved. Pour into a flat cake pan and let harden. Flavored gelatin could be used. These gelatin blocks are thick and can be cut and handled by the children for a snack. Cut in shapes using a knife or cookie cutter. Shapes and colors can be varied for holiday seasons.

3. Make sandwiches and cut them into shapes with cookie cutters or a knife.

4. Slice vegetables to show the shapes and patterns of each. Make a vegetable shape salad.

5. Pies, round cakes, and pizza are good for practicing with triangles.

6. In season, help the children make melon balls.

Activity 22

Seasonal Shapes

The seasons of the year provide many opportunities for discussing shapes. Some suggestions follow. Add to them and have the children help think of others.

Fall: Common shapes include leaves, acorns, squirrels, pumpkins, turkeys, etc. Use these shapes in art projects, cooking, and baking.

Winter: Common shapes for winter include snowflakes, snowmen, sleds (sleighs), and skates. Find pictures of winter scenes. Make pictures and collages using winter shapes (cotton balls for snowballs, snowmen, and snow clouds). If it snows, talk about the shapes of snowflakes and the shape patterns left on the windows. Build a snowman. Observe the shapes of the clouds on stormy days.

For the Christmas season, common shapes include stars, Christmas trees, a creche or manger scene, angels, ornaments (all shapes and sizes), wreaths, gingerbread children, and any other shapes that are part of the family Christmas celebration. Let the children help in all the family preparation for the holiday. Make it a learning time by talking about the shapes (colors and sizes) of the things used.

Spring: Common shapes include a cross, flowers, baby animals (ducks or chicks), hats, baskets, birds, and any other shapes which fit the family spring and Easter celebrations.

Summer: Some common shapes for summer are the sun, flags, balls, pail and shovel, ice cream cones, watermelon slices, and other shapes associated with vacations and summer fun. If you go to the beach, take along containers to use to make castles and other shapes in the sand.

Activity 23

Three Dimensional Shapes

When the children have a good working knowledge of shapes, begin to move toward three dimensional shapes. This may happen very early with some children or very late with others.

Children recognize three dimensional shapes early although they do not know the technical names or the relationship. As soon as they recognize a circle in a ball (sphere) or squares in their blocks (cubes), they are already beginning to grasp the concept of three dimensional shapes.

When the children ask, or when you feel the children have sufficient knowledge to make the associations, introduce the words sphere, cone, cube, and cylinder. Do this informally at first and introduce only one word at a time.

Treat these terms in the same way that the basic shapes were treated.

1. Have a "sphere hunt" or a "cylinder hunt."

2. Make charts or collages of things that can be found around the house and yard for each three dimensional shape.

3. Add these shapes to the shapes book and to the nature book or corner.

Final Note: Do not neglect the opportunities for learning that are all around you, on walks, in the park, at the store, in church, and in the car. Everything has a shape. This great variety should inspire unlimited ways for learning.

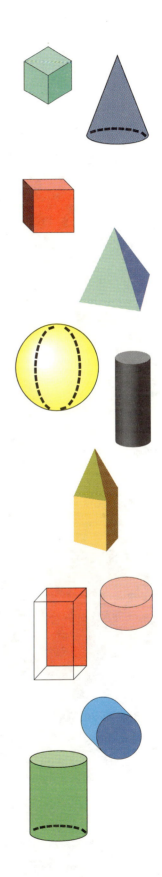

Section 3—Size

Introduction

"How big is baby?" "Soooooooooo big!"
This popular children's game is played very early
in children's lives, usually before they can talk or
walk. It can be used as a basis for the children's
understanding of size. From large to small and
from tall to short, everything has "size."

As with the concepts of color and shape, the
concepts of size and size relationships can be
introduced naturally and simply as
parents talk to and play with children.
When the children ask "what's that?" or
point at an object, the response might
include size as well as color or shape: "a big
red ball," "a tall tree," "a tiny speck of dust."

When reading picture books or stories to the
children point out size and size relationships.
"See the big dog!" "Look for the little puppy."
"Find the tall tree."

As the children's understanding grows ask
questions. "Can you find the bigger doll?" "Which
tree is taller?" "Which ball is smaller?"

When you go for walks or drive to the store have
the children spot tall, large, small, and short things
along the way.

At the park talk about the natural world and the
children's size relationship to the things around
them: trees, flowers, tables, etc.

In the playground section, compare sizes of swings,
slides, and other equipment with the sizes of the
children, an adult, or other things in the park. For
example, "Is the slide higher than a tree?" "Is
Mommy taller than the sand box?" "Does the seesaw go as high as a swing?" All of these concepts
can be developed naturally as part of the children's
early learning. They learn the vocabulary of size
as they learn about the world.

The activities and games which follow in this chapter begin with the very simple and progress to the more difficult. Read through the activities. Select those which fit your children's level of skills and interests. These are not formal lessons to be given on a specific day or time, but are to be given as the children grow in the knowledge of their home and the world around them. Coordinate them with similar activities in other sections.

Beginning Awareness

Before beginning the activities in this chapter and as children's awareness grows, begin to play a variation of the baby's "Sooooooo big!" game.

1. Have the children point to or hold different objects. Ask: "How big is the ball?" "Soooo big!" Help them approximate the size with their hands.

2. Ask about very large objects that will make children stretch their arms out wide. How big (or wide) is the sofa, the bed, the table?

3. Next try very small objects such as a button or a checker. Ask the children to show with their hands how small the object is. Now try even smaller objects (do not let the them put the objects in their mouth).

4. Find very tall objects such as a tree, the refrigerator, or the house. Ask the children how tall or how high the object is. They will have to stretch up high and reach to describe the object.

5. Find short objects like a step stool or a stuffed toy. Have the children stoop down to show the size.

6. Continue this game with them varying the concepts as their understanding grows. As their skills grow, add other concepts; long and short, thick and thin, wide and narrow, and so on.

7. When the children are old enough, let them lead the game and ask the parent, other children, or a friend to show the size of the chosen objects. As they progress, play more difficult games.

74

Find the Correct Size

1. Select an object such as a ball, a block, a cup, or a book.

2. Have the children find another object that is the same size as the first object. It may be the same type of object to begin with, but try to move the children to finding objects which are the same size, but not the same type. For example, at first have them find another cup that is the same size as the first cup, another ball that is the same size as the first ball, and so on.

3. When they can do this, have them find another object (a ball, a box, a block) that is the same size as the cup. This requires an estimate on the part of the children and will help them gage size relationships.

4. When the children can find objects the same size, make the activity more difficult by having them find another object that is bigger (or larger) than the object chosen.

5. Finally, have the children find an object which is smaller than the object chosen.

How BIG I Am !

Have the children do some size activities directly related to their own size.

1. Let the children search out five objects that are bigger than they are. Ask how they know that the objects are bigger. Have them try to demonstrate with their hands or body movements how much bigger the object is.

2. Expand the activity by asking the children how the object is bigger. For example, is the object "taller" than they are, or is it "wider" than they are, or is it "longer" than they are? This is a good way to introduce other size vocabulary and to help them demonstrate the differences in the meanings of these size words.

3. Repeat the first two steps with five objects that are smaller than the children. Introduce words such as "shorter," "littler," and so on.

Activity 3

Putting Objects in Order by Size

Provide a variety of materials which can be stacked or lined up according to size. Such items could include measuring cups which stack together, stainless steel or plastic mixing bowls, stacking (or "nesting") blocks, stacking (or "nesting") dolls, sets of wooden beads with large holes and varying sizes, or anything else that can be set out from small to large.

Have the children arrange the objects in the sets from smallest to largest and from largest to smallest. Allow them to string beads in the same pattern (small to large; large to small).

When the children can do this activity easily, begin to ask them questions about the sizes. Can they find a size in the "middle," one that is neither the largest nor the smallest?

Activity 4

Comparing Sizes

1. Place a variety of objects on the table or floor such as buttons, blocks, books, cups, beads, keys, bottle caps, or jar lids.

2. Ask the children to sort the objects by size. Use small bowls, egg cartons, divided foil trays, muffin tins, or other containers for sorting according to the size and number of objects used.

3. As the children sort the objects, talk about what they are doing.

   a. "Is the button, bigger than the block?"

   b. "Will the button fit on top of the block or will it fit better in a cup?"

   c. "Is the block larger or smaller than a cup?"

   d. "How many beads does it take to fill a cup?"

   e. "How many buttons does it take to fill the same cup?"

4. Encourage the children to find more than one way to sort the objects (color, shape, pattern).

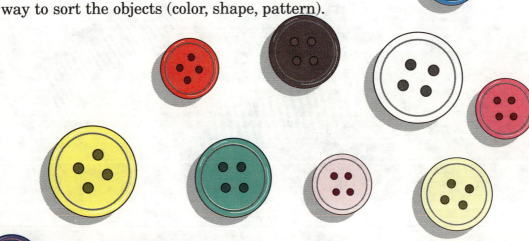

Activity 5

Extending Size Comparison Vocabulary

Extend size vocabulary throughout the house and into the world outside the home. As you go on walks or ride in the car, see what size descriptions and comparisons the children can find. If older brothers or sisters are with you, have them make up games that will help the younger children learn the different size words.

Here are some suggestions for objects and places which can be observed and used to help the children learn size vocabulary and concepts.

Big or little: People (adults or children), animals or birds (adult or young), cars, boxes, and almost any object made by God or man is in more than one size.

Large or small: Almost anything can fall into one of these groups. For example, insects, portions of food, and pots and pans.

Tall or short: People, buildings, trees, hills, statues, pitchers, and other things which are upright can be classified as tall or short.

Long or short: String, yarn, shelves, tables, or anything that can be stretched or measured laterally can be described as long or short. This concept may also be used to talk about time, as a long trip or a short walk. Comparisons can be made. A trip to the store may be short, but a trip to grandma's may be even shorter. A walk to the park may seem long, but a drive to another city can be even longer.

Thick or thin: Books, sauces, crayons, pencils, and slices of bread can be either thick or thin.

Wide or narrow: Ribbons, streets, rivers, lines are thought of as wide or narrow. Use the comparisons and activities found in *Activity Six* to reinforce these concepts. Have the children or parent create different games and activities.

Activity 6

Comparison Game

To extend the vocabulary for the size comparison of objects, select objects which come in varying sizes. Have the children repeat the correct terms for each group.

1. Three lengths of string to show
long		short
longer	or	shorter
longest		shortest

Use these strings for a size game in which the children find objects that are the same size as the string. Make a list of things that are the same size as each string. Put the string across the top of the page as a guide.

2. Three pencils of different lengths
long		short
longer	or	shorter
longest		shortest

3. A twelve inch ruler, a yard stick, and a measuring tape can also be used to demonstrate comparatives of long and short or tall and wide.

4. Use rubber bands of different thicknesses and have the children demonstrate which can be stretched the farthest or longest.

5. Use three or more glasses or vases to show tall, taller, and tallest.

6. Have the children find different size shoes (mom's, dad's, older children's, or their own) and line them up to show big, bigger, and biggest. Have them find three smaller shoes (their own, a baby's, or a doll's) and line them up to show small, smaller, and smallest.

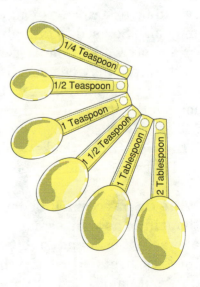

7. Find other materials such as three buttons, boxes, measuring spoons, and hats. Then ask the children what size words and comparisons they can find.

Puzzle Games

Make or purchase games of size comparison.

To make a size game:

1. Find or draw pictures of one object in three different sizes such as people, balls, strings, animals, cookies, apples, trees, chairs, and anything you can find or draw.

2. Glue the three pictures on a strip of tagboard or on half of a 5" x 8" file card.

3. When the glue has dried, cut the three pictures apart in a puzzle pattern. Choose a slightly different cut for each set so that the cards can only fit with those in their own set.

4. Mix up the cards and have the children reassemble them.

5. If you wish, print the words on the bottom or back of the card.

6. Store the cards in envelopes or in a small box.

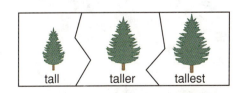

Activity 8

Size Bingo or Lotto

Making a simple bingo or lotto game:

1. Use four or six plain 5" x 8" file cards.

2. Divide each card into six equal sections.

3. Cut out or draw pictures of three pairs of opposites. For example, small or big cup, short or tall tree, baby or adult person or animal, big or small ball, long or short pencil, and thick or thin book. Make a different set for each card.

4. Glue the pictures to the card, using one picture for each section.

5. Make a matching set of individual cards. The easiest way to do this is to photocopy the completed cards, mount the copies on cardboard or a 5" x 8" file card, cover them with clear contact paper, and cut them apart. These cards can be used in three ways:

   a. As caller cards for bingo

   b. As matching cards for independent work

   c. As a memory game of finding opposites. See the directions for memory in *Color Section Activity Fourteen*.

Playing the game:

1. Shuffle the game cards and lay them face down on the table.

2. Give the player(s) buttons, beans, or small squares of paper to use as markers.

3. Parent or caller picks a card and calls out the picture on the card. For example, "one tall tree," or "two small books."

4. If the children have that picture on their card, have them place a marker on the picture.

5. When the card is filled, the game is over.

It is better to have at least two people play. It makes it more interesting for the children. Older children or the parent can easily call and play a card at the same time.

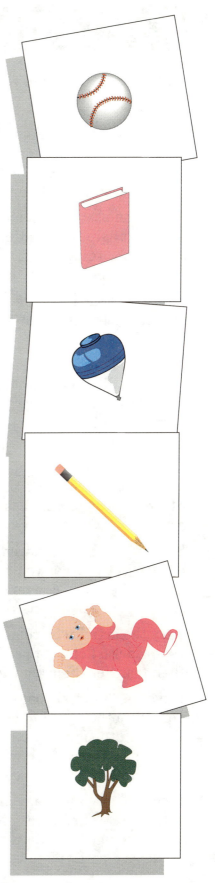

Activity 9

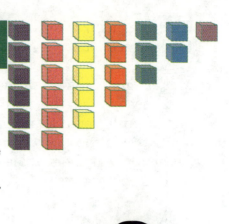

Pattern Games

1. Choose at least two sets of objects which can be arranged by size from smallest to largest. Use objects like buttons, different lengths of yarn or ribbon, blocks, beads, or measuring cups.

2. Spread one set of the objects on the table or floor and help the children to arrange the objects according to a size pattern: smallest to biggest, longest to shortest, biggest to smallest.

3. Talk about the arrangement. Ask the children to point to the smallest, the shortest, the largest or the biggest to make sure they grasp the vocabulary.

4. For more difficult comparisons, ask the children if they can find an object in the group that is bigger than the smallest one, but not as big as the largest.

5. Mix the objects again and ask them if they can arrange them in a size pattern you suggest. Start with something easy like biggest to smallest.

6. See how well the children can arrange the objects in the order you request without any help. When they can do this correctly, add a second group of objects from which to choose.

7. Vary the activity by removing either the smallest or largest object to see if the children can then transfer their knowledge to the new group.

8. Have the children choose a pattern for the parent or another child to follow. When they are secure in the activity, check their perception by setting up the pattern with one or two objects out of order to see if they can spot the problem.

9. Blocks of any kind may also be used for pattern activities. Set a pattern for the children to copy such as longest to shortest. Then have them make size patterns to be copied by others.

84

Activity 10

Nature Exploration

Nature provides an abundance of materials for talking about sizes and size relationships. Coordinate the nature activities here with those found in the color, shape, and size sections.

Explore the back yard, park, forest, seashore, or whatever natural surroundings are available.

1. Talk about "sizes" in nature.

2. Have the children find things to compare: different sized flowers, trees, seeds, leaves, rocks, and insects. Try to choose a different focus for each "exploration."

3. Take a magnifying glass along on one trip.

   a. Observe many things with the magnifying glass. See if familiar things look different. Can the children see fine lines on a leaf or flower petal that they could not see with their own eyes? Check many familiar objects and talk or write about the differences when you return home.

   b. Let the children check the area for things that are so small that they cannot be easily seen.

   c. If possible, collect some of these tiny creatures or objects using tweezers, and place them in a jar or container to be examined later in more detail.

   d. Make a chart or book about these tiny things in nature.

Activity 11

Sampling Nature

Most things in nature change size. Plants and animals grow. Hills, mountains, and rocks change more slowly through erosion. By helping the children observe the natural process of growing and changing around them, they reach an understanding not only of size, but also of the amazing world in which they live. After exploring nature, begin hands-on acivities.

1. In the fall, try to find seeds from flowers or trees. Discuss how the tiny seed grows into a flower or a tall tree.

2. Pick up samples of varying sizes of leaves, twigs, seeds, shells, and rocks.

   a. Use these objects to make nature collages.

   b. Mount samples of:

      1) A flower seed and the dried flower or petals.

      2) A tree seed (an acorn or seed from a pine cone), a dried leaf, and a photograph or drawing of the tree as it stands fully grown.

      3) Grains of sand and the rocks or shells from which it came.

Activity 12

Plants Grow and Change

1. Read a book which talks about the life cycle of plants. Talk about the process of moving from a seed, to a plant, to a flower, and back to a seed.

2. Write a story with the children about a tiny seed that grows into a tall tree, a beautiful flower, a weed, or whatever they find of interest.

3. Plant some seeds in a garden or in a pot. Have the children keep track of the change from the tiny seed to a plant.

4. Sprout some seeds in a jar or on a damp paper towel. Lima or kidney beans do well. Show the children how the seed opens and a tiny leaf emerges within a week or so.

MY PLANTS	
Day Planted	
Day Sprouted	
Day Leaves Opened	
Day Blossomed	
Day First Seeds or Pods	

Activity 13

Animals and Insects Grow and Change

Observe animals and insects with the children.

1. Use the magnifying glass to look for tiny insect eggs on leaves in the garden. Make sure the children look in safe places away from harmful insects and eggs.

2. Find books about butterflies and tadpoles which grow from a tiny egg into much larger things.

3. If possible, find or purchase a caterpillar and watch it grow in size, spin its cocoon, and change into a butterfly.

4. Read books about the growing cycle of other animals. Make a chart or collage of baby animals or baby and adult animals. Talk about the big change in size for some animals from baby to adult.

5. Take a trip to the zoo, science museum, or nature park.

    a. Talk about the different sizes of animals.

    b. Let the children make comparisons: animals that are bigger than the children, smaller than the children, or much taller than the children.

    c. Make a chart, book, or collage of animal sizes using some of the comparisons in *Activity Five* or let the children choose another "size" idea.

    d. Talk about how the small animals will grow. If possible, return to the zoo or park often to check on the growth of any baby animals. Do they get bigger quickly or slowly?

    e. If the children have a young pet, keep a record of its size as it grows.

Activity 14

People Change and Grow

After observing the changes in plants, animals, and insects, talk about the way people change and grow. Talk about the children's growth and the changes in their friends and relatives.

1. Talk about how they have grown.

   a. Look at baby pictures and records for height and weight.

   b. Compare them to their present size in height and weight.

2. Document the children's growth.

   a. Using butcher paper or large sheets of drawing paper, trace the children.

   b. Cut out the traced figures and have the children color them.

   c. Look in the children's baby records. Check how many inches long they were at birth and mark the number of inches on the traced figure.

   d. Ask the children to observe what "size" changes they have undergone since birth in regard to being taller, bigger, and heavier.

   e. Help the children to write a story telling about the changes they have been through. Emphasize that the changes not only include size, but also, and more importantly, changes in understanding, in learning, and in growing to be part of a family.

Activity 15

Using Stories in Comparison

To introduce comparative vocabulary, read stories which talk about size differences: fairy tales, such as, "The Three Bears," "The Three Billy Goats Gruff," or "Jack and the Beanstalk;" fables, such as the "Lion and the Mouse;" or Bible stories, such as the story of David and Goliath. These are a few of the many stories or poems that can be found to "teach" size words and comparisons.

1. Read the story with the children.

2. Have them tell the story back to you after sufficient reading time.

3. Let the children act out or draw the size comparisons as in "The Three Bears."

    a. Have them find a bowl the right size for Papa bear, Mama bear, and Baby bear.

    b. Ask the children to select chairs in the house that would fit Papa, Mama, and Baby bear.

    c. Ask them what would happen if Papa sat in baby's chair and *why* that would happen.

    d. Ask the children what it would be like to crawl into Papa bear's chair. Would they fit? Why not?

    e. Have them act out the story using dolls or stuffed animals that are the correct size for the characters.

    f. Ask the children how Goldilocks fits into the "size" picture of the story. Is she as big or tall as Papa or Mama? Is she bigger or smaller than Baby bear?

Use similar activities for other stories, fables, and Bible stories to help the children have a concrete picture of the size relationships. Use terms such as big, bigger, biggest and small, smaller, smallest so that they become familiar with the words.

Activity 16

Making a Size Book

When the children begin to comprehend size differences extend the activities. Making books, mobiles, collages, and charts is a good means to reinforce what is learned and to extend the ideas. Suggestions follow for each type of project. Choose those which interest the children and which will best help them.

1. Children like to make both big books and personal size books. The making of big books has been discussed in the *Color Section, Activity Seventeen*. Let the children choose the size. Subjects for books might be:

    a. Things larger or bigger than. . .

    b. Things smaller than. . .

    c. Things taller than. . .

    d. Things shorter than. . .

    e. Things the same size as. . .

    For the five suggestions listed, the comparison chosen can be the child or an object or person chosen by the child.

2. Other possibilities for books include:

    a. *Everything Has a Size.* This book could include many pages, each for a different size term. Or it could take different objects, such as, cars, trees, dolls, buttons, people, etc. Each page can be set up to show the variety of sizes in each group.

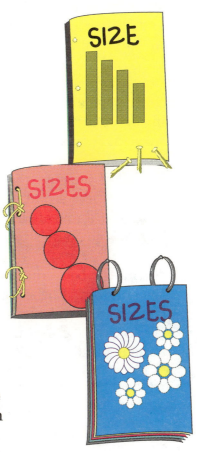

b. *Opposite Sizes*. This book could be set up so that facing pages show opposites: big or little, large or small, tall or short, long or short, thick or thin, wide or narrow. Let the children help choose the categories.

3. Once the focus of the book has been chosen:

a. Find pictures in magazines or catalogs to illustrate the theme.

b. Have the children draw pictures for the book to be used along with the cut pictures. These can be drawn directly in the book or drawn and cut out to paste in the book.

c. Choose the paper size for the book. Use slightly larger, heavier paper for the cover and laminate if possible. Clear contact plastic will help the covers last longer.

d. Carefully print the title of the book on the cover page and the subject headings on the inside pages. Help the children to read the words if they are interested.

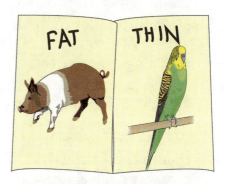

e. Put all of the pages together and sew or staple them like a real book. If staples are used, put a row of clear tape over the sharp edge of the staples to avoid pricked fingers.

f. "Read" the book and talk about it often with the children. Encourage them to make stories about the pictures and size relationships. Write their stories and add them to the book to be enjoyed or added to later.

Activity 17

Mobiles

Mobiles are always fun for children. They enjoy making mobiles and delight in watching them move once they are hung. A size mobile can be a good preparation for estimating and balancing skills.

1. Have the children draw a picture of themselves that is about four to five inches tall.

2. Cut out the figure and mount it on cardboard or heavy construction paper.

3. Color the back of the figure.

4. Hang this in the center of the mobile frame.

5. Have the children choose a theme:

   a. I am larger than. . .

   b. I am smaller than. . .

   c. I am taller than. . .

   d. Children's choice. . .

6. Have the children draw or cut pictures from magazines which are in proportion to the figure and the theme.

   a. If the children want to show things that are taller or bigger or larger than they are, then the pictures must be larger than the figure in the center of the mobile.

   b. If the figure is four inches tall, then the objects for the mobile will have to be more than four inches tall to show the actual size difference.

c. Help the children with the proportioning of the figures. If the object is in reality twice as tall as they are, then the picture of that object should be twice as tall as the figure of them (eight inches for a four inch figure). If the children choose very large objects, it may be wise to make their figure smaller (two or three inches).

d. Be careful to balance the sizes so that the mobile will hang evenly.

e. If, however, the children choose objects smaller or littler than themselves, then the pictures must be smaller (less than four inches for a four inch figure).

f. When the pictures are chosen, cut them out, mount them on cardboard or heavy paper, color the backs, and prepare to hang them.

g. Tie larger objects near the ends of the rods or sticks, balancing them carefully.

h. Tie the smaller objects at the middle of the rod or stick between the larger picture and the middle figure. Balance them.

This activity should help the children to gain some perspective of their place in the world.

For the most pleasing results you should carefully BALANCE your mobile.

Activity 18

Collages

This is another activity which will give the children some perspective on size.

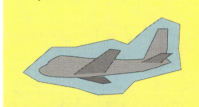

1. Pick an idea for a collage such as: big things, small things, tall things, wide things, narrow things, big or little, tall or short, I'm bigger than, I'm smaller than.

2. Have the children find materials for the collage which fit the idea chosen (sticks, yarn, buttons, pipe cleaners, drawings, pictures cut from magazines or catalogs).

3. If the children choose to be "in" the collage, have them draw themselves in proportion to the objects. Objects that are smaller than the children should be shown as smaller and those that are larger as larger.

4. Arrange and glue objects and pictures on a piece of heavy paper or cardboard.

5. When the collage is finished, neatly print the title on the paper (top, bottom, or middle). Print over the top of the pictures if necessary.

6. Help the children read the title.

7. Talk about the project just completed. Ask the children to explain what they have just done and what they have found interesting.

8. Hang the collage in a place where they will see it.

I am smaller than . . .

9. Talk about it on following days to reinforce the ideas learned.

10. Make up a story about the collage. Write it on paper and attach it to the back.

Activity 19

Charts

Making charts helps to develop and strengthen the children's organizing skills. Because of the number of concepts involved with understanding size, a variety of possibilities exist. Some suggestions follow. They are just that, suggestions. Use any variation that will help children to understand the concepts. Let them help think of ideas for a chart or try making a book of charts in which several concepts can be organized.

Activity 20

Geoboard Size Patterns

Use geoboard and pegboard activities to reinforce size concepts.

1. Make patterns on the geoboard for the children to copy.

2. Make a set of patterns on geopaper. Glue them to cardboard and cover with clear contact plastic for durability. The children may use these to work independently.

3. Have them make some patterns on the geoboard or on geopaper for an adult or other child to copy.

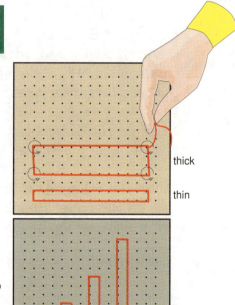

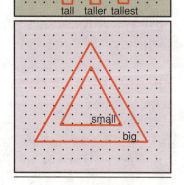

Activity 21

Experiments with Size

Size concepts are related to the measurement activities found in math curriculums on all levels. Activities for measurement will be found in the *Math Readiness Section Activity Six*. Some simple activity suggestions to prepare for measurement concepts follow. You may expand on these suggestions. The goal is to help the children to understand how size makes one container different from another.

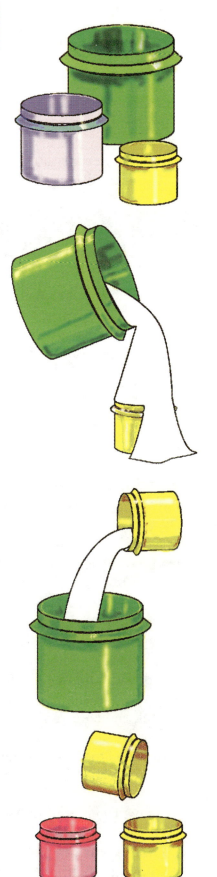

1. Give the children a variety of containers in different sizes: plastic bottles, bowls, cups, containers, pots, and pans. Plastic, stainless steel, or tin are better if they will be working without supervision. Glass containers should be used only with supervision. Be careful not to let the children break the glass and cut themselves.

2. Provide a work area for the children: sink, sandbox, any area which can be easily cleaned and controlled. A child's small swimming pool makes a good work space.

3. Provide materials like water, sand, dried beans, or rice for the children to fill the containers. Rubber dishpans, large plastic storage containers, large cooking pots, or large stainless steel bowls make good "holders" for these materials.

4. Have the children choose one of the empty containers and fill it.

   a. Ask them to choose another container that might hold the same amount.

   b. Have them pour from the first to the second container. What happens? Is the second container too big, too small, or just right?

   c. Next ask the children to choose a larger container. How many small containers will it take to fill the larger container?

d. Choose a large container for the children. Have them fill it. Select a smaller container. Let them carefully pour the material from the larger container into the smaller container. What happens? How many small containers can the children fill with the material in the larger container?

e. Let them continue to experiment with the remaining containers.

Activity 22

Art Activities

These activities involve art and art materials. Use them as projects to reinforce size concepts.

1. Have the children draw or paint a picture of their family showing the size relationships. Talk about their finished picture. Who is the tallest? Who is the smallest? Who is taller than whom?

2. Use painting, drawing, or sculpting with clay or play dough to reinforce any of these concepts.

3. To emphasize size relationships, give the children two pieces of paper. This activity can be repeated with each combination.

a. Any one of these:
one very large and one very small,
one long and narrow and one short and wide,
one tall and one short.

b. Ask the children what they can draw on the large (long, tall) sheet that they cannot draw on the small (short) sheet. Talk about things which could fit on either sheet.

c. Have the children draw a picture on each.

d. Talk about the pictures and any problem they had fitting the picture on the smaller or shorter sheet.

Activity 23

Cooking and Size

Use time in the kitchen to help the children learn more about size. Many kitchen activities are a preparation for or actual practice in the measurement concepts covered in the *Math Readiness Section*.

1. When using a recipe to bake or cook from scratch, let the children help measure the ingredients. Ask, "Which measuring cup is larger?" "Which measuring spoon is used to measure very small amounts?"

2. Put out three different bowls instead of one. Ask the children to pick the one they think is big enough to make the recipe. Have all the ingredients nearby so that the children can make a fair guess. This helps prepare them for estimating activities.

3. Let the children cut pieces of cake, pie, or pizza for the family. Have them see if all the pieces are the same. If not, which piece is bigger? Which is smaller? Which is the smallest?

Activity 24

Seasons and Size

Using the topics for the seasons listed in the *Color Section Activity Twenty-three* and *Shape Section Activity Twenty-two*, create games or art projects for the concepts learned in this section.

Fall:

1. Compare the sizes of:

   a. Leaves that fall off the trees

   b. Pumpkins in the fields or grocery stores

   c. Turkeys in the stores for Thanksgiving

2. Make families of pilgrims and Indians helping the children to find the appropriate size for each member of the families.

3. Make a lotto game of various size pumpkins, turkeys, etc.

Christmas season:

1. Cut out many stars in various sizes. Cover them with foil or paint them with glitter and hang them in windows or on the Christmas tree.

2. Talk about the sizes of Christmas trees in the lots, in the stores, and in the homes of friends.

3. Make several different sizes of Christmas cookies or candies.

4. Talk about the sizes of ornaments while decorating the tree and the house.

Winter:

1. Make several sizes of snowmen and snowflakes out of white construction paper. Use these to make size pattern games or make game boards with matching figures and use like lotto.

2. Make similar activities using hearts near Valentine's Day.

3. Make mobiles or collages using any number of winter shapes.

Spring or Easter:

1. Make memory games or lotto games using different sizes of flowers, chicks, ducks, birds, or hats. Arrange objects, in pairs like two small flowers, two big ducks, two tall hats for the games.

2. Use any of the activities in this and other sections with the seasonal topics to give a new emphasis (books, mobiles, posters, charts, and games).

Summer:

1. Use patriotic themes and summer activities as a basis for size activities.

2. Let the children help pack picnic lunches and decide on the meal size (portions and amounts) needed for the family. Let them cut the watermelon into different size pieces.

Conclusion

Size, like shape and color, can be learned from the things around the children in the world in which they live. Materials to teach these concepts are everywhere.

Most teaching supply stores and some department stores carry workbooks that give more formal worksheets to check or reinforce the concepts learned here.

As always, use what is available and what interests the child. A simple drive to the store, to church, to the park, or a friendly visit can be a rich learning experience.

Section 4—Position and Direction

Introduction

You stand *on* the floor. You sit *on* the chair. You climb *over* the wall or fence. You walk *up* or *down* the stairs. Position or direction words are often essential to getting a point across to small children.

There are five keys to teaching these and all other basic concepts to young children.

1. Talk to children, even when they are babies, in complete sentences. Examine the language used with babies and small children. Words for position or direction occur frequently: "Come *to* Mama." "Get *down*." "Sit *on* my lap." "Come *back* here!" "Pick me *up*!" "Come *over* here." "*Down*!" ("Put me *down*!") "Put your shoes and socks *on*."

Many more examples can be given. To evaluate your children's abilities, make a list. Add to it all the position and direction words used by both parent and children.

2. Answer early questions.

3. Read to the children every day.

4. Use everyday activities and surroundings to help the children understand the vocabulary.

5. Play games which will help them to understand these position and direction concepts long before they make a formal connection or can demonstrate on paper what each word means.

"Acting out" activities will easily and naturally reinforce position and direction concepts as children grow and will help them to understand the precise meaning of the vocabulary. These activities can be combined with stories, rhymes, fables, and Bible stories.

Position and direction words and concepts are usually considered in pairs or groups (up and down, over, under and on). The first three pairs of position and direction words are presented in detail. The other pairs of position and direction words will be presented in less detail with suggested activities specific to the pairs. Familiarity with the first pairs of position and direction words is helpful in the understanding of the pairs and groups presented later. Hands-on activities and art projects will be used to reinforce each concept. The art projects may be displayed or made into a "Position and Direction Book" to be used for review, for fun, for making up stories, or for a variety of other projects inspired by the children.

Remember to use any learning opportunity that presents itself. Take a walk, a ride in the car, a trip to the grocery store or mall, a bedtime story, a day of baking and cooking, or any other event to teach and reinforce a concept.

Read through the activities and select some which suit the children's abilities, needs, and interests. Have them act out as many activities as possible and use as many manipulatives as needed to portray and reinforce the concepts.

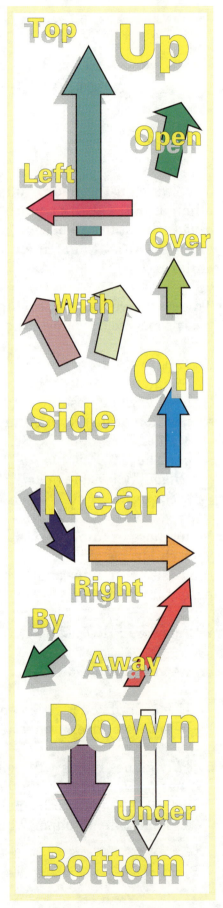

Right and Left Activities

Learning *right* and *left* is often difficult for children. Parents should begin early to use the terms *left* and *right* in everyday situations. "Let me hold your *left* hand." "I'll put on your *right* shoe first." "Put the block in your *left* hand." "Can you hop on your *right* foot?" This type of informal learning will make it easier for children to distinguish *left* from *right*.

Note the children's preferences and let them work from their dominant hand (*right* or *left*). Do not try to force them to use one hand rather than the other.

Activity 1

Reading Left to Right

Start by showing the children that when a book is opened, the pages are read from left to right. Move on to the reading of a single page.

1. Point to the text as it is read.

2. Show the children that the words on the page are read from the left side of the page to the right side of the page.

3. Have them follow along for several pages. This will help them to prepare for reading. Take the opportunity to remind them how to handle a book with care.

Show the children a calendar grid which shows the days and the dates in a left to right progression. Have them mark off the days for a week or a month in succession as they occur.

Activity 2

Finding the Right or Left Objects

Have the children try to find the right or left object.

1. Select pairs of objects (bears, blocks, keys, bottle caps, buttons, spoons) and place one object from each pair along the right side of the table. Then place the matching object along the left side. *For young children line the objects up in the same order on each side until they are familiar with the game. As they progress, mix the order of the objects on each side.*

2. Ask the children to select an object from the right side of the table. Then ask them to select a matching object from the left side of the table.

3. As they gain confidence in matching, ask more difficult questions which use concepts learned in other sections.

    a. For a blue block say: "Find a square, blue object on the right (or left) side of the table."

    b. For a green marble or ball say: "Find a round, green object on the left (or right) side of the table."

4. Have the children give directions to the parent or to an older brother, sister, or friend. Choose most of the items requested from the "correct" side of the table. In one or two cases, however, make the selection from the "wrong" side of the table. See if they can catch the "mistake."

5. When walking or driving, talk about right and left turn lanes on the road. Show the children that an arrow usually points out the direction that is allowed. Have them spot the left turn arrow on stop lights when available. As they progress, have them look for signs with the words Right Turn and Left Turn.

106

Activity 3

Making a Right and Left Book

Your children will enjoy making a special cloth book with right and left pages. The book for this section can be a special "act out" book.

Start by covering several pieces of large cardboard or tagboard with felt. Next, trace and cut out several shapes from felt or material scraps which will adhere to the felt boards.

1. Cut out several people figures that are both children and adult size to use throughout the book.

2. Cut out several birds, and small animals. Make one or two house shapes, one or two trees, some hills, some clouds, a sun, some cars, planes, fences, or balls. All these shapes are good for "outdoor scenes."

3. Cut out some simple "indoor" shapes as well: a table, a bed, windows, a door, a counter, a stove.

4. You may want to have the children trace their hands and feet on felt, cut them out, and place them on the appropriate sides of the pages.

Write a title in big letters. For example: Position and Direction Book; My Book of Ups and Down, Ins and Outs, and Other Things; or any title the children can think up which is appropriate. Let them help decorate with pictures of the different position and direction concepts as they are learned. Next punch three holes spaced evenly down the side of the cover and the felt covered pages. Lace yarn or ribbon through the holes or use metal chart rings to hold the book together. Finally, keep the felt shapes in a pocket or envelope attached to the back of the cover. It may be helpful to refer to *Activity Eighteen* in the *Shape Section*.

107

Now that the book is made, as each position and direction concept is introduced, use the felt pages as story boards to "act out" the new words.

Using the shapes you have made, act out right to left and left to right scenes.

1. Have the children set up an outdoor scene with the shapes.

2. Then show them how a bird may fly from right to left. Have the children repeat the action.

3. Make up simple stories in which people, cars, and animals move from one side of the page to the other.

4. As the children become more confident with right and left, give more specific directions. Put the car on the left side of the house. Move the child to the right side of the tree.

5. Finally, let the children give the directions and make up stories.

Specific uses for this book will be given after each group of position and direction words.

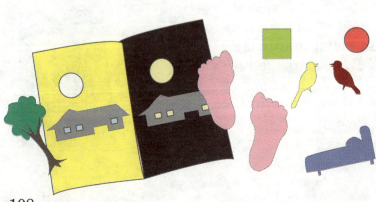

FELT BOOK story example:

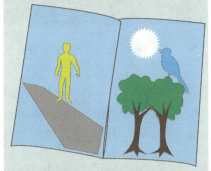

The sun was high UP IN the sky when Bobby came DOWN the street. A bird IN the trees sang a happy song.

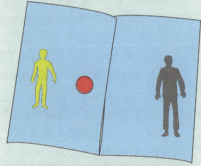

"What a great afternoon to play with my big red kick ball!" said Bobby. He asked his dad to come OUT of the house. Bobby went to the LEFT side and his dad went to the RIGHT side. Later they traded places.

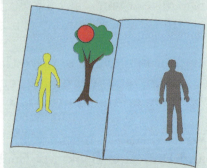

They kicked the ball ACROSS the yard until Bobby kicked it too HIGH. UP,UP, UP the ball soared, and got caught IN a tree.

Dad went INTO the garage and got his ladder. He climbed UP and brought Bobby's ball DOWN. Then they went IN and had a good dinner.

Activity 4

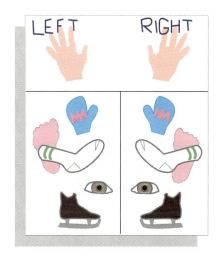

Making a Chart for Right and Left

Print the words "left" and "right" at the top of a large sheet of construction paper or tagboard. Trace a child's right hand on the right side of the chart and his left hand on the left side of the chart. See example at the right.

Using the chart:

1. Have the children draw or find pictures of things that they do with each hand or that come in right and left pairs such as mittens, shoes, and skates.

2. When the chart is completed, it may be displayed or it can be used as the first page in a large Position and Direction Book.

3. Have the children make up right and left hand stories: "What if all mittens were left-handed?"

Activity 5

Right Hand Turkey

Creating Art Projects for Right and Left

Help the children trace their right and left hands on a sheet of paper or let them dip their hands in paint and make hand prints.

1. Have the children think of birds or animals that could be made from these hands.

2. Try the same activity with the right, then left, foot. The children may enjoy using the hands and feet animals to make a colorful mobile to hang in their room.

3. Make a plaster cast of each child's hands and feet. When the plaster is dry, paint or decorate.

Left Foot Moose

Activity 6

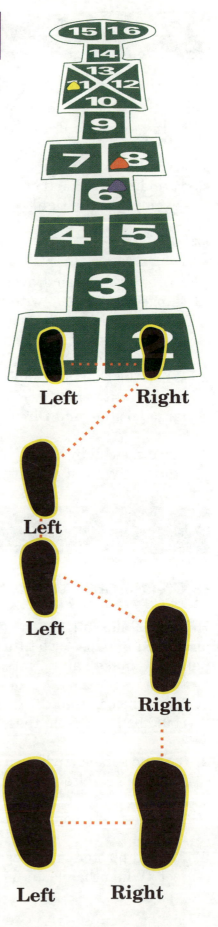

Right and Left Games

Playing games helps to establish the right and left concept. Play "Here we go Looby Loo," "Simon Says," or invent your own games.

1. Have the children use only the right hand for activities such as playing ball, or building a house. Use the left for the next activity.

2. Find pairs of shoes, mittens, gloves, or other right and left pairs. Ask the children to find all those that would fit on the left foot or hand. Now mix the pairs and ask them to find those that would fit the right foot or hand.

3. Play "Simon Says" using only left and right commands: "Put your left hand up." "Hop on your right foot."

    a. The children are to obey all commands which begin with the words "Simon says."

    b. Any command that does not begin with "Simon says," should not be followed.

    c. The parent or teacher should also use commands not prefaced with "Simon says": "Close your mouth." "Hop on one foot."

    d. If the children obey the command without "Simon says," the game is over. Practice with the mixed commands so that the children understand what they are to do.

4. When they gain some accuracy and confidence, have them give instructions to a parent, to a brother, or to a sister for right and left games.

5. Extend the activity to things outside: "What can you see out the right or left side of the car?" "Should we sit on the left or right hand side of the church?"

110

Up and Down Activities

Up and *down* are learned very early. Children want to be "picked *up*" or "put *down*." Toddlers hold their arms out to be picked *up* and squirm when they want *down*.

If toddlers live in a home with stairs, they learn to climb *up* and *down* with varying degrees of success. They will attempt to climb any object higher than themselves if a desired object rests at the top.

The phrase "*down!*" or "get *down!*" can be heard frequently at this stage of development, uttered either by a frustrated parent or stranded children.

For all of these reasons, reinforcing *up* and *down* should not be difficult.

Activity 7

Up and Down with Favorite Toys

1. Help the children to construct steps with their building blocks.

    a. This can be difficult because of the balance required for some blocks. If linking blocks are used, balance is not a problem, but the construction can be difficult for young children.

    b. When the steps are constructed, let the children take small toys (bears, dolls) and march them up and down the steps.

    c. Have them build steps for a house or bridge and act out stories about people or animals that need to go up into the house or come down to get out of the house.

2. If the children have stacking cubes, let them build a tower so that a small toy can be used to climb up to the top and back down again.

Activity 8

Up and Down the Elevator, Escalator, and Stairs

1. Go to a store, mall, office building, parking garage, or any building that has an elevator, stairs, or escalator.

2. Have the children try to figure out which sign or button they must push to go up an elevator, and which to go down. Signs differ and they may need some help the first time. If they recognize the words "up" and "down," encourage them to read the signs and to find these words near stairs or escalators. Signs usually are one of the following types.

    a. There may be buttons to be pushed which say "up" and "down." In most cases the children will need to know that to go up, they must push a higher number. To come down, they must push a lower number.

    b. Signs or symbols may say "up" or "down." Sometimes directional arrows are used.

c. Braille signs and verbal clues are used. Let the children feel the symbols for up and down in those elevators which have braille signs. Talk about the braille and why it is there. Most elevators in newer buildings are also combining voice clues as well, such as "up," "down," or giving the floor number.

3. Ask the children to think about what would happen if people tried to go "up the down escalator" or "down the up escalator."

4. After several times using and talking about elevators, escalators, and stairs, have the children draw pictures using the different signs they have learned for "up" and "down."

Activity 9

Things That Go Up and Down

The following activities could be used to introduce several science concepts as well as extending children's understanding of up and down.

1. Talk to children about things that go up and down. How many things can they list? What things only go down (rain, snow)?

   a. Ask the children to name things that they can toss up into the air (a ball, rock, small object). What happens? Do they stay in the air? Do they come down? Why?

   b. Do some things stay in the air (a helium filled balloon) or come down very slowly (a feather or a leaf)? Why?

2. Go to the library and find books about things that go up and down. Try to find a book that tells why things that go up usually come down.

3. Fly a kite. Talk about what is needed to keep the kite up in the air (wind, air currents), and why the kite comes down (not enough wind or air current).

4. Go to an airport and watch the airplanes take off and land. Try to talk to someone who knows about planes and can explain simply how a plane goes up to fly and comes down to land.

5. Go to the park and use the swings, slides, seesaw, and any other park equipment which utilizes up and down motion. Observe what is needed for children to go up and down.

   a. Swings need to be pushed and pumped.

   b. Children need to climb up a slide before sliding down.

   c. Two children about equal in weight are needed for a seesaw.

114

Activity 10

Demonstrating Up and Down

When the children have completed some or all of the up and down activities, make a chart, poster, collage, or drawing to illustrate what children have learned about up and down. These can be displayed in the children's room, or in a Position and Direction Book made like the book in *Colors Section Activity Seventeen*.

1. Have the children draw or find a picture of things that go up and down or signs and symbols which tell people to go up or down.

2. Take the drawings and pictures and arrange them on a chart, collage, or on separate pages.

3. Cloth Book ideas: Add a ladder, a set of steps, or an elevator to the set of felt shapes made in *Activity Three*.

   a. Use the felt pages to create scenes in which the children can first see and then demonstrate the concepts of up and down.

   b. Stories help develop understanding. Children should eventually make their own stories for up and down.

Activity 11

Up and Down Rhymes and Stories

Have the children learn and act out nursery rhymes which use "up" and "down."

1. *Eentsy, Weentsy Spider*
   Eentsy, weentsy spider went up the water spout.
   Down came the rain and washed the spider out.
   Out came the sun and dried up all the rain.
   An eentsy, weentsy spider went up the spout again.

2. *Jack and Jill*
   Jack and Jill went up the hill
   To fetch a pail of water.
   Jack fell down and broke his crown,
   And Jill came tumbling after.

3. *Hickory, Dickory, Dock*
   Hickory, Dickory, Dock
   The mouse ran up the clock.
   The clock struck one,
   The mouse ran down.
   Hickory, Dickory, Dock.

4. *The Grand Old Duke of York*
   The grand old duke of York,
   He had 10,000 men.
   He marched them up the hill.
   And he marched them down again.

   Now when you're up you're up
   And when you're down, you're down
   And when you're only half way up
   You're neither up nor down.
   (This can be done at different speeds.)

5. *Jack and the Beanstalk* Read the story of Jack and the Beanstalk. Have the children act out the story and then draw Jack climbing up the beanstalk and the giant chasing him down.

6. Find and read other stories, fables, or Bible stories which use up and down as part of the story. Have the children act out the story with toys or puppets and draw pictures of the up and down parts of the story.

High and Low Activities

The activities for *high* and *low* follow easily after those for up and down. *High* and *low* refer to the position something reaches when it is up (*high*) or down (*low*). When a kite or plane is up in the sky, it is very *high*. On the other hand, when the kite or the plane "lands," it comes down *low* to the ground.

High and *low* also are related to the activities for tall and short in the *Size Section Activity Six*. Something which is *high* such as a tree, a building, or a stairway is generally tall. Something which is *low* such as shrubs and flowers is generally short.

Activity 12

How High Can I Go?

Assemble several objects which can be thrown safely into the air: a small rubber ball, bottle cap, button, leaf, feather and flower. Go outside and mark a spot for the children to stand. The spot should be in relation to something tall, such as a tree (not too close, but near enough so that the children can gage how high each object will go). Demonstrate what the children are to do.

Do this activity first on a very calm day. Repeat on a windy day and compare the results.

1. Pick a light object such as a leaf, feather, or flower and throw it as high as it will go. How high does it go? Does it go higher than the tree, just about as high, or not quite as high?

2. Throw an object such as a button, bottle cap, or small toy that is heavier than those in the first group but not as heavy as a rubber ball as high as it will go. Did it go higher than the lighter object? Did it go as high, higher, or not as high as the tree?

3. Repeat the experiment with the ball, having the children throw it as high as they can. Now have them bounce the ball gently at first, and then as hard as they can. How high does the ball go?

4. Make further observations concerning:

   a. Which objects come down the fastest? Why?

   b. Which objects come down very slowly? Why?

Then check books from the library to find simple answers. Let the children give their own ideas about why these things happen.

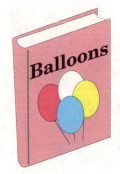   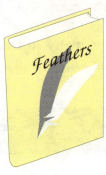 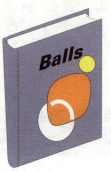

Activity 13

UP HIGH

1. THE SUN

2. AIRPLANE

3. BIRDS!

4. THE SKY

5. CLOUDS

6. RAINBOW

7. A BIG TREE

High and Low as We Go

This activity may be done in two stages (high, low) over several days.

1. When taking a walk with the children, take along a pencil and paper so that they can dictate all the things they see that are high above them and all the things that are down low.

2. Focus on four areas to list from top to bottom:

   a. Things the children can see such as sky, sun, and clouds.

   b. Things that are higher than the children such as mountains, buildings, trees, a house, or a very tall person.

c. The lowest thing the children can see such as the ground, a valley, or a ditch.

d. Things the children see that are lower then their knees such as flowers, grass, shrubs, pets, or insects.

3. To help the children relate to what they saw, make a collage, chart, mobile, or diorama of the things that were higher or lower than the children. Use drawings, pictures cut from magazines or catalogs, things made from pipe cleaners, scraps of materials, or anything which fits the object to be shown. Label the activity and talk about it with the children.

Activity 14

High as the Ceiling—Low as the Floor

Repeat the steps in *Activity Thirteen* inside the house.

1. Have the children stand in a room and find:

    a. The highest thing in the room (ceiling) or near the ceiling (fans, lights, pipes).

    b. The things higher than the children's heads (walls, windows, pictures).

    c. The things in the house (room) that are lower than their knees.

2. Ask the children if they can think of anything in the house that is higher than the ceiling (attic) or lower than the floor (basement).

3. Record all of the children's responses as in *Activity Thirteen*. Use some of the previously suggested activities to document and review the high and low things in the house.

Activity 15

Sing High—Sing Low

High and low are also used to describe sound. The differences are not difficult for children to hear, but they are difficult to explain. Choose some simple books at the library to help. Try a few simple experiments.

1. Begin with simple sound experiments. Play or sing two notes for the children. Ask which is higher. Repeat several times varying the num-

120

ber of notes and the pattern: high, low; low, high; high, low, lower; low, high, higher; high, low, higher. Let the children take turns playing or singing the notes.

2. Take five glass containers. Vases, jars, or drinking glasses of the *same* size may be used.

    a. Fill each container with a different amount of water.

    b. Gently strike the glass containers and compare the sounds. Adjust the levels of water so that something close to a musical scale is achieved.

    c. Have the children observe which containers make the lowest and highest sounds.

    d. Change the arrangement of the containers. See if the children can arrange them high to low or low to high by listening to the sounds as they strike each container.

3. If a stringed musical instrument is available, let the children experiment with the sound of the different strings.

    a. Show them that the thicker the string or wire, the lower the sound.

    b. Let the children try plucking the string.

    c. Have them place one finger high up on the string and hold it down firmly while plucking the string with a finger on the other hand. What change do they hear? Is the sound higher or lower?

This sound experiment can be done with different sized rubber bands, with tightly pulled strings of varying thicknesses, with rubber bands strung on a geoboard, or with pins driven into a board at different depths.

Activity 16

Book Activities for High and Low

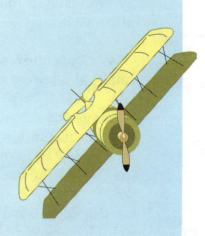

1. Make a "high" page and a "low" page to add to the Position and Direction Book mentioned in *Activity Ten*.

2. Cloth Book. Use the pages in the special cloth book made in *Activity Three* to introduce and reinforce high and low.

   a. Use shapes to make indoor and outdoor pages.

   b. Use shapes to show a bird high in the sky or a person high on a ladder.

   c. Have the children show the bird flying low, or a person low on the ladder.

   d. Make scenes for them to repeat.

   e. Have them eventually make their own scenes and stories to show high and low.

Over, Under, and On (Above, Below) Activities

As the opportunities arise, point out to the children the relationship between *over* (above) and *under* (below). *On* is used here to contrast with *over* and *under*. It is used in the sense of resting *on* the surface of something in contrast to being either *over* or *under* something.

Activity 17

Experiments and Practice with Over, Under, and On

1. Do some science experiments with objects that float (corks, feathers, empty plastic bottles) on the surface of the water and others that sink under the water.

2. Give the children practice in using these concepts in daily activities. Have each of them sit on a chair, the floor, or a bed. Let them put some food on plates, crawl under a table to retrieve a toy, or put a placemat under the plate.

3. Make a list with the children of all the ways they use over, under, and on (above and below) in one day's time. Have them illustrate their favorite activity for each concept.

4. Make up stories for the concepts. "Things Hiding under the Bed." "What Happens over our Heads?" "Let's Go Walking on a Tightrope."

Activity 18

Over, Under, and On Games

Play games in which the children must go "over," "under," or "on" something:

1. Play leap frog (over).

2. Play variations of "Simon Says" using over, under, and on.

3. Place a line or rope on the ground. Have the children jump over the rope. Gradually raise the line so that they must jump a little higher each time.

4. Tie or hold a line or rope for the children to crawl under. Gradually lower the line so that they must stoop down to crawl under.

5. Using the same line or rope, have the children bounce or throw a ball over the line. Later have them roll the ball under the line.

6. Create an obstacle course in the house, yard, or at the park. Have several things which the children can go under, over, or walk on.

7. Play games in which they toss, hit, or throw a ball over a net, chair, or other object.

8. Draw a chalk path on the sidewalk or driveway. Have it go in a straight line for a few feet, then twist and turn in various directions. Ask the children to walk on the line. Besides reinforcing the concept of "on," this will aid in the evaluation of each child's progress in balance and tracking skills.

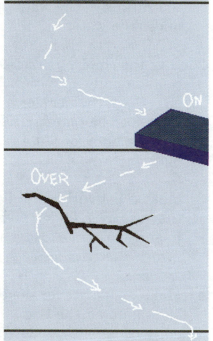

Activity 19

Rhymes, Stories, and Games for Over, Under, and On

Act out rhymes or stories such as, "Jack Be Nimble" and "Hey Diddle Diddle" to illustrate the concept of *over*, "Twinkle, Twinkle Little Star" to show *above*; "Little Boy Blue" (*under* the haystack); and "Humpty Dumpty" (sat *on* the wall).

Activity 20

Book Activities for Over, Under, and On

1. Have the children make pages in their Position and Direction Book.

2. Sample activities for the special cloth book:

   a. Arrange the cloth page so that one or more objects such as a street, a hill, a tree, or a house cross the middle of the page.

   b. Using the other figures, give the children instructions for placing these figures over (above), under (below), or on the central objects. Put a bird in the sky over the house. Put a child under the tree. Put another bird on the roof of the house.

   c. When the skills are more advanced, have the children create a scene or story using over (above), under (below), plus all of the position and direction words learned to this point (right and left, up and down, high and low).

On and Off Activities

The words *on* and *off* have two different usages for the children.

1. *On* is used in *Activities Seventeen* through *Twenty* in the sense of something or someone physically being *on* a chair, road, line, or table. This sense also applies to something being physically taken *off* the table, chair, or someone physically getting *off* of the chair, sofa, bed, or other object. It is further used with reference to putting *on* (or taking *off*) socks, shoes, or clothes.

2. *On* and *off* are also used in the sense of turning a light, an appliance, a car, and similar things *on* or *off* in *Activities Twenty-One* through *Twenty-Three*.

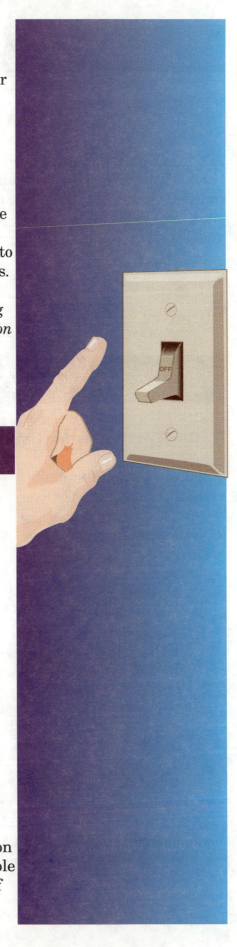

Activity 21

Experiments with On and Off

1. Discuss the different ways in which things can be turned on and off: switch, plug, key, and so on.

2. Show the children a flashlight with no batteries. Turn the switch. What happens? Put in the batteries and try again. What happens? Talk about the words "energy" and "power" as they are understood by the children. Use this as a base to talk to the children about why things go on or off when the switch or key is turned. See if they can think of different sources of power for things such as electricity, batteries, gasoline, natural gas, or the sun.

3. Go to the library and find some simple books on why and how things work. Have them available for the children to look through. Read some of the easier ones to them.

4. Go through the house or classroom and find all of the things which can be turned on and off.

   a. Using words, pictures from magazines, or those drawn by the children, make a list of the items.

   b. Divide the items into groups: those which have a switch, those which need a key, etc.

   c. Talk about each item and what makes it go on: batteries, electricity, gas, or other.

Activity 22

Rhymes, Stories, and Games for On and Off

1. Review and act out rhymes or stories which use on and off. "Polly Put the Kettle on," "Diddle, Diddle, Dumpling."

2. Play variations of "Simon Says" using on and off. Include items such as "Simon says take your right shoe off." "Simon says put your socks on."

3. Play musical chairs or some variation in which the children do an activity while the music is on but must freeze in position when the music is turned off.

4. Discuss different things which the children can get "on to" and "off of" such as a bus, a train, a plane, or a merry-go-round. Talk about safety rules for getting on and off of moving objects.

Activity 23

Book Activities for On and Off

1. Here are some ideas for charts, collages, or drawings to be put in the Position and Direction Book mentioned in *Activity Ten*. Things That Turn On and Off; Things We Put On; Things We Get On; or Things We Take Off.

2. Add stories to the book dealing with on and off: "The Day All the Lights Went Off" "The Machine That Would Not Turn Off."

3. Try additional ideas for the cloth position and direction book found in *Activity Three*. Use the cloth shapes to create stories or scenes involving on and off.

   a. Have a cat sitting on a fence or on a roof. Let the cat jump off the fence or roof when the dog begins to chase it.

   b. A child sits on a chair to do school work and gets off when mother calls for dinner.

   c. Encourage the children to create their own scenes and stories for on and off.

Open and Close Activities

Open and *close* (or shut) are terms which children hear very early. "Please *close* the door," is a sentence spoken often by parents as their toddlers go in and out of the house.

All children are very eager to *open* presents or a package of cookies.

As always, begin with the everyday use of the words involved and build from there.

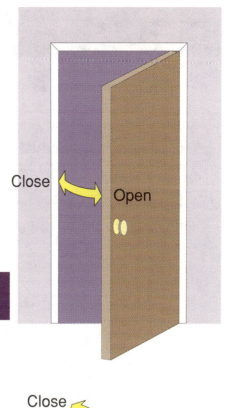

Activity 24

Exploring Open and Close

1. Begin with eyes, mouth, or hands, since these can be opened and closed. Play "Simon Says" or a similar game to see if the children understand these words: "Simon says, open your eyes." "Simon says, close your mouth." "Simon says, open and close your left hand."

2. Talk about all of the objects in the house or classroom which can be opened and closed: doors, windows, drawers, boxes, bottles, jars, and any others the children suggest. Make a count of all the objects which can be opened and closed. For example, how many doors (include all doors in the house, even refrigerator doors) and how many windows?

3. When shopping, have the children find "OPEN" and "CLOSED" signs in store windows. See if they can tell what hours a particular store is open and when it is closed. Does the store have open and closed signs in other languages?

4. Have the children think of some things which they would try to open, but not try to close such as nut shells or presents.

Activity 25

Book Activities for Open and Close

1. You may wish to make the open and shut house (see illustrations) and use it as a page in the Position and Direction Book in *Activity Ten*.

2. Use the cloth book made in *Activity Three* to demonstrate the opening and closing of a book.

   a. Place a scene inside the book.

   b. Close the book. What happens to the scene?

   c. Open the book to show the scene.

   d. Have the children think of other ways to show open and close using the shapes. For example, place a shape inside the door or window of the house. Close the door or window. Have the children open the door or window to reveal what is inside.

Open and Shut Activity

Use the house below for a pattern to trace and color. Carefully cut open the windows and the door on the dotted lines, and use the solid lines as hinges. Paste or glue the house to tagboard. Be careful not to glue the windows or the door shut!

You may affix the figures (found at the bottom of the page) inside the windows of your house, or you may wish to make your own figures. Try a standing stick figure for the front door.

In and Out (Inside, Outside and Indoors, Outdoors) Activities

As with all position and direction words, children use *in* and *out* every day. They like to crawl *in* and *out* of big boxes, run *in* and *out* of the sprinkler in summer, crawl *in* and *out* of bed each day. They need to adjust clothing when the temperature *outside* is different from that on the *inside*.

Tell the children that sometimes inside can be called indoors and outside can be called outdoors. Can they figure out why these words might be used?

Activity 26

Exploring In and Out

1. Talk about the different ways in which children use "in" and "out" each day. Ask if they can think of some other words for "in" and "out" which are used very often such as entrance and exit. Help the children to recognize and associate these words with "in" and "out."

2. Play games such as "Go in and out the window" with them.

3. Find books which visualize the concepts.

4. Draw or cut out pictures of things inside the house. Contrast this with a collage of pictures of things found outside the house.

5. Make a list of places where children go in and out: doors, houses, church, stores, the shower, and the bathtub.

6. Search the house or classroom and find where children can put things in or take things out: drawers, washing machine, dryer, or toy box.

7. Talk about turning things inside out. Find things which can be turned inside out.

Inside/Outside My House	
Inside	Outside

131

Activity 27

Book Activities for In and Out

1. Some ideas for the Position and Direction Book made in *Activity Ten*:

    a. Places we go in and out

    b. Inside things

    c. Outside things

    d. Inside and outside clothes

2. Some more ideas for the cloth book made in *Activity Three*:

    a. Have the children use the shapes to create an outside scene on one of the pages in the cloth book. Have them point out those things which can only be found outside.

    b. Have the children use a second page in the cloth book to create an inside scene or story. Have them point out those things which can only be found inside.

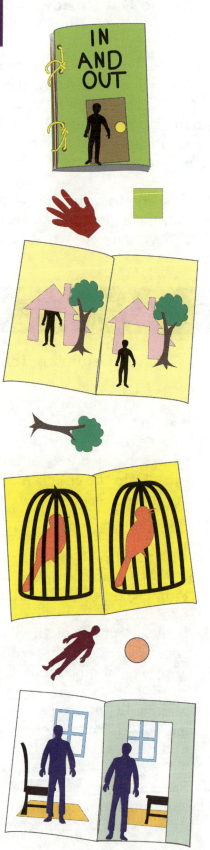

Front and Back Activities

The idea of *front* and *back* is often confusing for young children. Getting clothes on the right way takes time for many children. Use the following activities to introduce or reinforce these concepts for them.

Activity 28

Exploring Front and Back

1. Talk about things which have a front and a back: books, clothing, money (coins and bills), toys, dolls, cars, buses, stores, houses, papers, people, and almost anything else the children encounter each day.

2. Talk about front and back locations: front yard and back yard, front door and back door.

3. Have each child find five things and point out the front and the back of each object.

4. Ask the children how they can usually tell the front of their clothes from the back (labels).

5. Spend time with a book. Show the children how they move from the front to the back of a book when they read.

6. Talk about standing in line at school, the grocery store, the bank, or the library. When the children stand in line, they must move from the back of the line to the front.

7. Purchase or make a front and back memory game.

Activity 29

Book Activities for Front and Back

1. Ideas for the Position and Direction Book made in *Activity Ten*:

   a. Front and back

   b. Places I stand in line

2. Additional ideas for the cloth book made in *Activity Three*:

   a. Have the children create either an indoor or outdoor scene.

   b. Ask the children to show a line of people or animals waiting to get into or out of a place in the scene. Have them point out those people or animals at the front of the line and those at the back.

   c. If the scene is an outdoor scene, ask the children to place certain shapes or people in the back of the house (tree, car, and so on). Then have them place other objects in the front of the house.

   d. Have the children create their own scenes or stories to demonstrate front and back.

Before and After Activities

Before and *after* are similar to front and back because things will usually fall *before* (in front of) or *after* (in back of) something else in relationship to other things. They differ in that front can mean the very first in a series and back the very last in that series.

Learning *before* and *after* is important for learning sequencing in both language arts and math.

Activity 30

Exploring Before and After

1. Discuss things that the children do in terms of before and after.

   a. *"Before* we go to the park, we must stop at the store."

   b. "What shall we do *after* we go to the park?"

   c. "What should you do *before* you go to bed?"

   d. "Wash your hands *before* meals."

   e. "We will play a game *after* we clean up toys."

2. Let the children suggest before and after situations which they use each day.

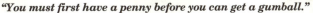

"You must first have a penny before you can get a gumball."

Activity 31

Demonstrating Before and After

1. Have the children find or draw pictures which show several before and after scenes:

   a. Messy room or clean room

   b. Run-down house or painted, repaired house

   c. Clean baby before eating ice cream or messy baby after eating ice cream

   d. Rainy, muddy yard or dry yard

   e. Balloon blown up or balloon burst

2. Use a large calendar for the month. Mark down important events for the month. Pick a date like the fifteenth. What events will happen before that date? Which will happen after that date?

3. Write the date of the present year on a paper or chalk board. Write the previous year and the following year on either side. Ask the children to point out this year's date, then the date of the years before and after. Read the numbers.

4. Children are very interested in family history. Talk about family events which took place before and after the children were born (weddings, births of older siblings, birthdays, special anniversaries, births of younger brothers and sisters, and special events).

5. Use cooking time to reinforce before and after.

   a. Ask the children to tell all the steps needed before they can bake some cookies (getting out all the ingredients, getting out the cooking utensils, getting the recipe ready, turning on the oven).

b. Emphasize also the order in which ingredients are put together. Which ingredient must come before the others?

c. After the ingredients are mixed and the cookies placed on the sheets in the oven, have the children help with the chores which must be done after the cookies are made. Let them put the ingredients away, clean up the dishes, and put out a cooling rack for the cookies.

d. Apply this to other cooking activities as well.

6. Use manipulatives (blocks, marbles, bears, buttons, toys, any small hands-on materials) to set *before* and *after* patterns:

a. Set out two blocks and a bear. Ask the children to put the bear before the two blocks.

b. Put one block before the bear and the other block after the bear.

c. Now put the bear after the two blocks.

7. Create more complicated patterns as the children's skills and understanding increase:

a. Take five objects such as two blocks, two bears, and one boat.

b. Ask the children to put the boat before the two bears, but after the two blocks.

c. Ask the children to put one bear before the two blocks, the second bear after the two blocks, and the boat before the first bear.

Activity 32

Before and After—Context and Meaning

1. Read a familiar story to the children and then close the book.

   a. Selecting one main event of the story, ask the children to recall what happened before and after it.

   b. Initially, stay with things that happened in the book.

   Cinderella
   What happened to Cinderella before her sisters left for the ball?
   What happened to Cinderella after her sisters left for the ball?
   What would happen to Cinderella after midnight?
   Who tried on the glass slippers before Cinderella?

2. As the children mature, ask more speculative questions; those which require the children to imagine what went on before the story in the book and what might happen to the characters after the story in the book has ended.

   Possible questions about what happened before:
   What do you think Cinderella did before her father married the wicked stepmother?
   How did Cinderella dress?
   What games might she play?
   Was she happy or sad?

   Possible questions about what happened after:
   Where did Cinderella and the Prince go to live?
   Were they kind to the people in their kingdom?
   Why do you think so?
   Do you think they had children?
   Were the children boys or girls?
   What were the children's names?

138

Activity 33

Book Activities for Before and After

1. Here are some Position and Direction ideas to add to the book made in *Activity Ten*.

   a. Illustrate before and after scenes.

   b. Draw a central character from a story in the center of the page. Decide on a specific important event in the story. Divide the page from top to bottom around the figure (see illustration). On the left side of the page, draw what happened to the character before the event. On the right side of the page, draw what took place after the event.

   c. Pick a specific event or chore. Make a list of words or pictures of all the steps needed before the event or chore can be done. List the things which must be done after the event or chore is finished.

2. Here are some cloth book ideas to add to the book made in *Activity Three*.

   a. Tell the children a story using the shapes from the cloth book.

   b. Ask them to create a scene on one page showing something that might have happened before the story.

   c. Ask them to create a scene on another page showing something that might have happened after the story.

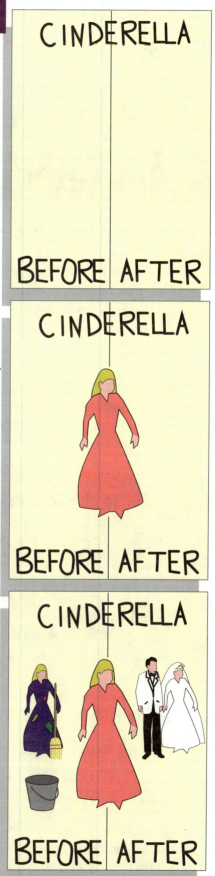

Beginning, Middle, and End (First, Middle, and Last) Activities

Beginning, middle, and *end* are closely related to the concepts just learned (front and back, before and after). The added dimension is the *middle,* the concept of something coming between two points.

Activity 34

Exploring Beginning, Middle, and End

1. Talk about beginning, middle, and end with the children. Let them give ideas about things which are familiar to them. They may suggest things such as a story, a song, a day (morning, afternoon, evening), or a book.

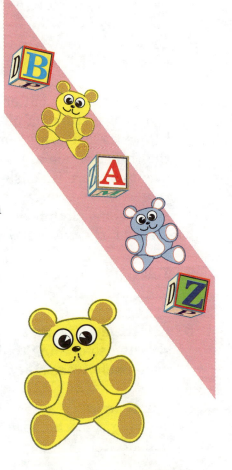

2. Using blocks, bears, buttons, marbles, or small toys, demonstrate beginning, middle, and end. Using an odd number of objects, set a pattern for the children to copy.

   a. Take three blocks and two bears. Line them up in an alternating pattern.

   b. Find the block at the beginning.

   c. Find the block at the end of the pattern.

   d. Find the block in the middle. Point out that the middle block has the same number of objects (two) on either side.

   e. As the children become more proficient, use more difficult patterns and more objects.

3. Using the same objects, give the children instructions for making patterns.

   a. Take one bear, one block, and one marble.

   b. Put the bear before the block and after the marble. (Pattern illustrated on next page.)

140

c. Point to the object at the end (block).

d. Point to the object in the middle (bear).

e. Point to the object at the beginning (marble).

As the children advance, give them more difficult directions or let them give directions to someone else.

4. Show the children a book.

a. Find the beginning and the end of the book.

b. Help them find the middle of the book by having about the same number of pages on the right and on the left. Start with books having only a small number of pages.

c. Have the children examine several books to find the beginning, middle, and end.

5. Use a calendar with twelve months on one page.

a. Talk about some holidays during the year.

b. Mark holidays on the calendar with stickers.

c. Ask the children to name the holiday that comes at the beginning of the year (New Year's) and one near the end of the year (Christmas).

d. Ask them to find a holiday which comes in the middle of the year (Father's Day or July Fourth). To locate the middle of the year, show them that about the same number of months comes before and after the holiday.

6. Take a large calendar of a single month.

a. Find the beginning or first day of the month.

b. Find the end or last day of the month.

c. Find the middle of the month, a number that is about the same number of days from both beginning and end.

Activity 35

Practicing Beginning, Middle, and End

1. Take short comic strips (three to five frames). Read and discuss them with the children. Cut the frames apart and scramble them. See if the children can pick out the beginning, middle, and end frames and put them in order.

2. Review familiar stories, nursery rhymes, or songs and ask the children if they can tell what happened in the beginning, in the middle, and at the end of each one. Have them act out the scenes.

3. Reinforce "middle" with games such as the "Farmer in the Dell," "Monkey in the Middle," or "Here we go round the Mulberry Bush" by having a child stand in the middle of the circle. When the games are finished, have all the children stand in a straight line and decide which child is in the middle of the line.

4. Talk about things which are in the "middle" or times when children find themselves in the middle. For example, the line down the middle of the road, the middle seat in a car or van, being in the middle between two dolls or two adults, being in the middle between an older and a younger brother or sister.

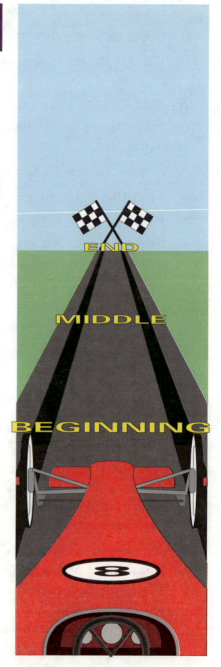

Book Activities for Beginning, Middle, and End

1. Ideas for the Position and Direction Book made in *Activity Ten:*

   a. Draw the beginning, middle, and end of a favorite story.

   b. Divide the page into three sections. Label them and find or draw pictures which show the beginning, middle, and end.

2. Ideas for the cloth book made in *Activity Three*:

   a. Use three pages of the cloth book to create a story in three parts.

   b. Using the shapes, have the children suggest story ideas.

   c. Choose one idea and have them tell how the story will begin, what will happen in the middle, and the ending for the story.

   d. Using the story pages as a guide, write the story down and keep it to be read often.

Beginning

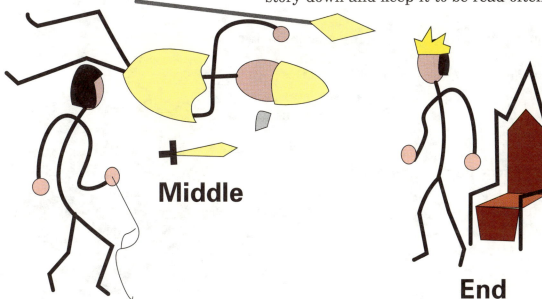

Middle

End

Top, Bottom, and Side Activities

The final word groups covered in this section are *top*, *bottom*, and *side*. These concepts can be related to others in the section. Any three-dimensional object can be used to demonstrate these concepts.

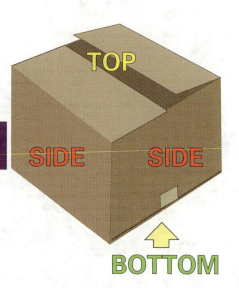

Activity 37

Exploring Top, Bottom, and Side

1. Take a large box.

   a. Ask the children to point out the top, the bottom, and the side of the box.

   b. Turn the box on its side. Again ask them to point to the top.

   c. How many children can still identify the top of the box when it is turned sideways?

   d. Turn the box upside down and have them identify each position.

   e. Ask the children how they know which is the top, the bottom, and the side.

2. Repeat the activity above using a large picture.

3. Move on to other objects familiar to the children: tables, chairs, stairs, glasses, cups, clothing, and toys. Let them find things to use as examples.

4. Play "Simon Says" using these words: "Put your hand on top of your head." "Put your left hand on the bottom of your right foot." "Put both hands on your sides.

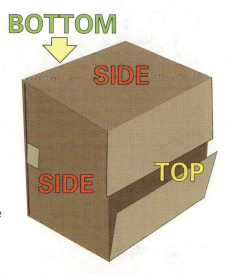

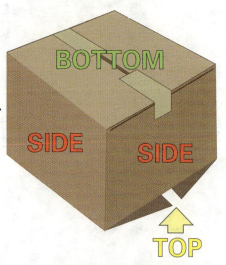

Activity 38

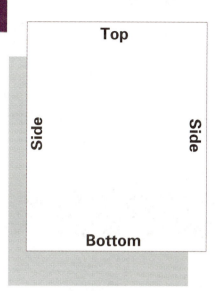

Book Activities for Top, Bottom, and Side

1. Ideas for the Position and Direction Book made in *Activity Ten*:

   Label a large sheet of paper or tagboard at the top, on the bottom, and on the sides. Have the children choose an indoor or outdoor scene and draw or cut pictures that would fit on each section of the page.

2. More ideas for the cloth book made in *Activity Three*:

   a. Do several directed activities. Instruct the children to place certain shapes at the top of the page, others at the bottom, and still others on the side. Have the children explain why each shape fits where it has been placed.

   b. Repeat the activity above, but place some shapes that do not belong in each section to see if the children can spot those which are out of place. Have them give a reason why these shapes should not be where they are. For example, ask them to place a cat in the sky, a cloud on the ground, or a chair on top of a house. Now have them tell why the location is wrong.

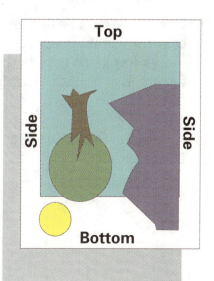

   c. Have the children create stories and scenes which demonstrate what they have learned about top, bottom, and side.

Review Activities for All Position and Direction Concepts

The following activities serve as reinforcement and review for all of the previous concepts. Many concepts may be integrated into one activity. You can use these activities as supplements for any weak areas the children have.

Activity 39

Reading Books and Poems

Reading books together is a good beginning for learning any concept. Start when the children are very young. As the children begin to respond and ask questions or point out things in the stories and pictures of the book, talk about the pictures.

1. Point out the positions of things. "The sun is *in the sky* (or *high in the sky*)." "The dog is *under* the tree." "The boy is *behind* the door."

2. As the children's understanding grows, move on to asking them simple questions. For example, "What is *under* the tree?" "Who is *behind* the door?" "What is *in* the dog's mouth?"

3. Gradually make the questions more difficult so that they must give the position word answer. For example, "Where is the boy?" (*under* the haystack). "What is the dog doing?" (catching a frisbee *in* his mouth).

4. Finally, as the children are able, let them ask the questions of the reader.

Activity 40

Coordinating Activities

Extend the "acting out" of position and direction words by returning to the easier activities found in the colors, shapes, and sizes sections. For example, using the "find" or "hunt" activities in these sections (*Colors, Activities Two* and *Three*; *Shapes, Activity Two*; and *Sizes, Activity One*), have the children find a specific color, shape, or size *inside* a cupboard, *under* a table, *on top of* a bookcase, and so on.

Activity 41

Simon Says

Play "Simon Says" using a variety of position and direction words. Add more difficult words as the children gain confidence and understanding:

> Simon says put your hand on your head.
> Simon says jump up high.
> Simon says stoop down low.
> Simon says open your mouth.
> Simon says close your eyes.
> Simon says put your hands over your head.
> Simon says put your right hand under your chin.*

*The last command is more difficult and should be used only after the children begin to understand right and left. Add more difficult concepts as they progress in their learning.

Activity 42

A Game of Opposites

When the children have grasped most of the concepts in this section, play a game of opposites. This can be done in different ways and used at different times for review.

1. Present a direction or position by acting it out, describing it, drawing, or by finding a picture for it. Examples: up, over, high, closed, front.

2. Have the children identify the position or direction presented.

3. Ask them to act out, describe, or find a picture for the opposite position or direction. For example: down, under, low, open, back.

4. This activity can be done in various ways throughout the section to judge the children's understanding of the concepts presented.

5. Let them take the lead when they are able.

6. When they begin to tire, *stop* and resume later or on another day.

Activity 43

The Position and Direction Game

1. This activity can be done on a large sheet of paper, on a chalk board, or in the cloth book. All three may be used at different times to review.

2. In the middle of the paper or board sketch a house. In the cloth book, place the house in the middle of one of the pages.

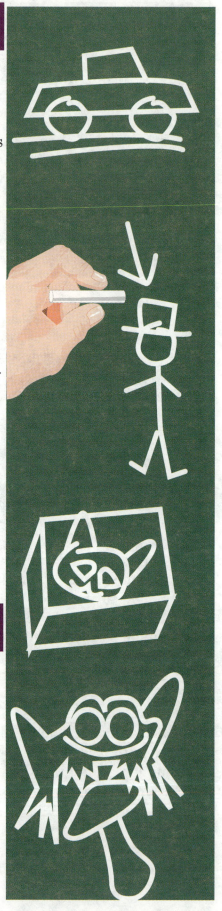

3. Direct the children to add to the picture following your specific directions. Try to include as many position and direction words as possible:

a. Draw a bird flying over the house.

b. Draw a sun up in the sky.

c. Draw a path in front of the house.

d. Draw a tree next to (at the side of) the house.

e. Draw a closed door at the front of the house.

f. Draw an open window.

g. Draw flowers on the right side of the house.

h. Draw a dog under the tree.

i. Draw a fence on all sides of the house.

j. Draw an airplane flying high in the sky.

k. Draw a person in the middle of the garden.

l. Draw a butterfly flying low over the flowers.

m. Draw a dirt pile at the back of the house.

n. Draw children sliding down the dirt pile.

4. This activity may be done over several days if the children tire easily. Review any areas in which they seem to be confused.

5. Let them choose or draw a central picture and give directions to another child or an adult.

As with all activities in all sections of this book, do not overlook the opportunities around the home, the car trip, the nature walk, the park, the museum, the zoo, and all areas where the children spend the day. These areas provide rich learning materials for all concepts.

Section 5—Matching and Grouping

Introduction

Everyone and everything has a place in the world and fits into more than one group or category. Children learn to place objects into groups at a very early age. Young children learn quickly that some objects can be put in the mouth while others cannot. They learn that one group of objects can be touched while another cannot.

Children begin to "match" or "group" things as soon as they can choose two objects with a common characteristic. When they can find two objects of the same color, shape, or size, they have begun using the skills which will allow them to make more formal distinctions later.

To check the children's simple matching skills, *Activity One* contains some review of the matching activities found in earlier sections. If they still have difficulty matching, repeat those activities which stress the areas of difficulty.

As the children move toward kindergarten and a more formal school experience, they will need more specific activities and games to develop the skills in one-to-one correspondence and in putting objects into groups or categories. These skills help them to understand how people and things around them "fit" into their world (family, class in school or church, age, human race, and girl or boy).

This section begins with simple matching to reinforce activities in previous sections and moves to activities which stress one-to-one correspondence and grouping. Everyday activities can be used to teach and reinforce these skills. The children should have mastered the more common groupings (color, shape, size) by the time they enter kindergarten. Many children, however, will be ready to tackle more complex groupings. *Some activities are difficult because they involve the basics of logical thinking.* Some children may not be able to "figure out" or solve all of the grouping problems until they are a little older. Others may not yet have the visual perception to "sort out" the differences in specific groups. If the children find an activity too difficult or tiring after trying hard, *stop* and rest or go on to something else. Return to the activity at a later time when they are ready to try again.

As always, use whatever is at hand. Do not neglect the world outside the home and classroom. Use field trips, walks, and trips to the grocery store and church to reinforce and expand the learning of the concepts taught.

Let the children participate in creating activities. Ask them to choose groups of objects they see and explain how these objects fit into one or more groups.

Read through all the activities and choose those which fit the needs and skills of the children. *Do not feel obligated to follow the order in the section or to do all of the activities. Do feel free to adapt the activities to the needs of the children and to create new ones.*

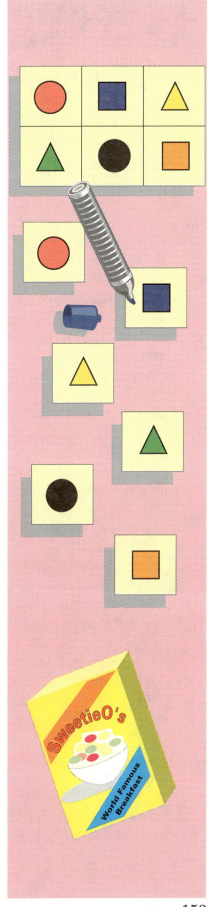

Activity 1

Simple Matching

1. Check the matching activities from other Sections.

   a. *Color Section–Activities Two, Thirteen, and Fourteen*

   b. *Shapes Section–Activities Ten and Fourteen*

   c. *Sizes Section–Activity Eight*

2. Play memory, bingo, or dominoes with the children to review simple matching skills.

3. Use card games to review matching.

   a. Play a game such as Old Maid which has pairs or Animal Rummy which usually has sets of four matching cards. Play the games according to the rules or simply lay out the cards as a matching practice and let the children invent their own matching game.

   b. Use a deck of Uno® cards and have the children match all the four's, two's, and ten's. Invent games which require matching pairs or four of a kind.

4. Match items in the grocery store.

   a. Show the children a can of food or a box of their favorite cereal at home.

   b. Have them look for the "matching" can or box at the grocery store.

5. In department stores, have the children find other household items or toys which "match" those at home.

6. On walks, have them try to find matching leaves, seeds, flowers, etc.

Activity 2

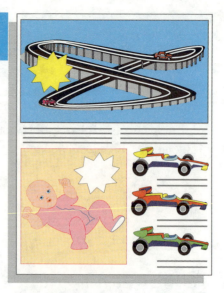

All Purpose Matching

This matching activity can be used for simple matching as well as for grouping and one-to-one correspondence. You can use catalogs, magazines, or old calendars.

Catalogs

1. Find two identical catalogs. If the catalogs are very large, divide them into sections so that they are manageable.

2. Cut the first catalog apart and file the separate pictures in envelopes or a file box. These pictures will be used for matching activities.

3. Keep the second catalog whole or with sections intact to be used as a "workbook."

4. To begin with section on simple matching, use single pictures cut from the first catalog.

   a. Give the children a picture of a car, a doll, or a kitchen item.

   b. Have them find the section of the catalog in which the picture will be found. This is good preparation for later grouping activities.

   c. Ask them to find the picture in the second catalog which matches the picture given them from the first catalog. Help them until they fully understand the activity.

5. When children become skilled at this, set up a "treasure hunt" for them.

   a. To start select five or six pictures from different sections of the catalog.

b. Ask them to search the catalog and find the section and then the corresponding pictures for each one. Give them slips of paper or some type of bookmark to show where the picture is in the catalog.

c. When they have found all of the pictures, give them a "prize." Let them set up a treasure hunt for someone else or let them choose a game to play.

6. Encourage the children to invent ways to use the catalog and its matching pictures.

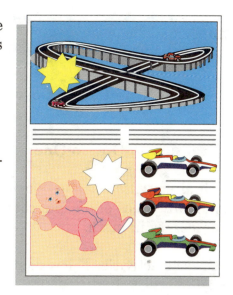

Magazines and Calendars

1. Begin by selecting two *identical* magazines or calendars which have large pictures. Calendars are good for very young children because they have only one picture per page.

2. Cut the first magazine or calendar apart into separate pictures. Cut full page pictures into four or five large shapes and place in individual envelopes or folders. Play puzzle games with the children using the full page pictures.

3. Keep the second magazine or calendar whole to use as the workbook.

4. Follow steps four, five, and six described under catalogs to finish the activity.

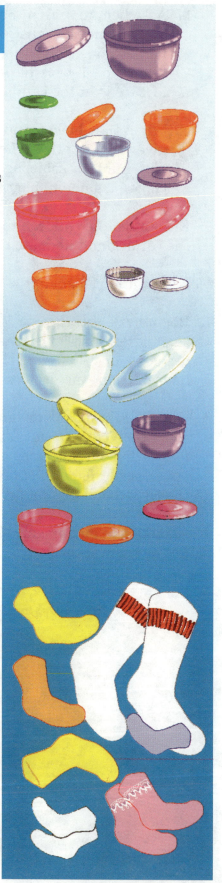

Activity 3

One-to-One Correspondence

Practice In One-to-One

Children will need one-to-one correspondence skills in many areas of life, but they will be especially necessary in math.

Use the activities below to strengthen these skills.

1. Put out an assortment of plastic bowls and lids for the children. Have at least three or four different sizes. Initially, make sure that the bowls and the lids match.

    a. Have the children match the correct lid with each bowl.

    b. As they progress, use more bowls than lids.

        1) Match the correct lid with each bowl and discuss why all bowls where not used.

        2) Then bring out the remaining lids for the children to match.

2. Choose several pairs of socks from the whole family. First separate the pairs and mix them all together. Have the children find the mate to each sock. Next match the socks to the family member who wears them.

3. Do similar activities with nuts and bolts; cups and saucers; pots, pans and lids; mittens; pairs of shoes; and any other items which require two things that go together.

Activity 4

Do We Have Enough?

Another aspect of one-to-one skills is the ability to judge the correct number of items needed for a specific event. Consider the following activities and add others with the children's help.

1. Ask the children to count the number of people who will be eating supper.

   a. Check to see if each person will have a chair to sit on. If not, have them supply the number of chairs needed.

   b. Set the table for the correct number of people. This means that they will have to choose the correct number of:

      1) Placemats

      2) Napkins

      3) Knives, forks, spoons

      4) Plates, cups, other dishes

   Vary this activity by setting out the materials needed for the children. Initially, set out the correct number. When they set the table easily and correctly, put out varied numbers of each item. For five people, put out four forks, five spoons, three knives, and five napkins.

   Let the children set the table and ask them to spot what is missing so that each person has one of each item needed.

2. For further practice make or purchase workbooks or worksheets which give the children valuable practice in one-to-one correspondence.

Activity 5

Grouping

Objects, subjects, and even people are often divided into groups or categories based on common characteristics. The children have already experienced some grouping activities, such as those in the colors, shapes, and sizes sections. The nature activities of the colors, shapes, and sizes sections also provide grouping practice when they put together different leaves, seeds, and rocks.

Review grouping activities from previous sections.

1. *Colors Section– Activities Seven, Eight, Nine,* and *Fifteen.*

2. *Shapes Section– Activities Eight, Sixteen, Seventeen,* and *Eighteen.*

3. *Sizes Section– Activities One, Four, Ten,* and *Nineteen.*

Activity 6

Finding Large Groups

Have the children find groups of items around the house, in the classroom, and outside which have common characteristics. Their selection is endless. Look for *broad* categories, not those with fine distinctions. Have the children find other examples.

Around the house

Furniture
1. chairs
2. beds
3. lamps
4. tables

Kitchen equipment
1. pots
2. bowls
3. baking pans
4. cooking utensils
5. dishes
6. silverware

Food
1. fruits
2. vegetables
3. cereal
4. meat
5. canned foods
6. packaged foods
7. frozen foods
8. desserts

d. Clothing
1. socks
2. shorts
3. shirts
4. skirts
5. trousers
6. dresses
7. coats
8. jackets
9. night clothes

In the Classroom

Toys
1. blocks
2. dolls
3. games

Books
1. picture
2. story

Art supplies
1. smocks
2. paint
3. brushes
4. easels
5. crayons
6. chalk
7. paper

Naptime supplies
1. mats
2. blankets
3. storybook

Science corner (items will vary)

Housekeeping corner (items will vary)

Outside the home or classroom

Playground equipment
1. swings
2. slide
3. jungle gym

Vegetation
1. flowers
2. trees
3. bushes
4. grass

Things to watch for
1. birds
2. dogs
3. cats
4. other animals

Things to collect (with permission)
1. leaves
2. seeds
3. rocks
4. interesting sticks

Activity 7

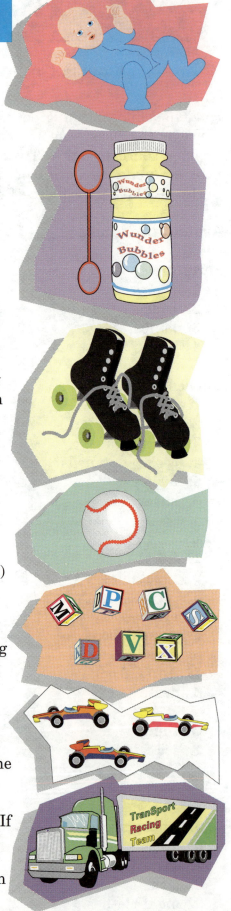

Where Does It Belong?

Use the catalogs from *Activity Two* in this section for a variety of other activities:

1. Begin with a section of the catalog which the children will readily recognize, such as the toy section or the clothing section.

2. Use the "workbook" or uncut section to talk about all the different items.

   a. Talk about how some items fit together: dolls, cars, trucks, balls, books, games, and stuffed animals.

   b. Let the children point out groups that they see. Accept anything which reasonably can be called a group.

   c. Have them tell you why some items fit in one group and not another. For example, why would a doll fit in with toys? Why would not that same doll fit in with cars?

This will help the children begin to understand that something may belong to a large group (toys) and a small group (dolls) at the same time.

3. When the children are comfortable with this kind of grouping activity, put the uncut catalog section aside.

   a. Take out the envelopes with the pictures from the cut catalog.

   b. Choose a section of the catalog and have the children spread out all the pictures.

   c. Ask them to put the pictures into groups. If a picture seems to be misplaced, ask them why they chose to put the picture in that particular group. Accept any logical reason the children give. If necessary, guide them to the most logical place for the picture.

4. As the children master one section, try other sections of the catalog. Do this activity once or twice a week along with the other activities.

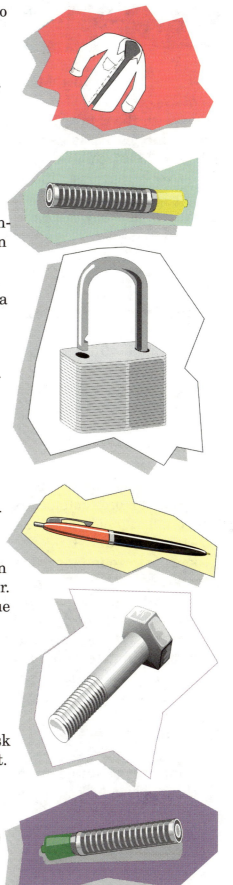

5. When the children begin to sort the pictures easily within a section, begin to do more difficult activities. Take pictures from more than one section and mix them. Some children should be able to sort the pictures first into general groups (toys, utensils, etc.) and then within each group.

   If possible, do these sorting activities in an area where the pictures can be left. If the children tire of sorting, return to it later.

6. Use some of the cut pictures and have the children make their own catalog.

   a. Have them choose the sections they would include in a catalog.

   b. Allow them to pick the pictures from each group that they would include in their catalog if they could be the "catalog maker."

   c. To make the catalog, use a notebook or plain paper. Staple or tie the plain paper together. Help the children label each section and glue or tape in the pictures they have chosen.

7. Go through other catalogs.

   a. Discuss the sections.

   b. If the catalog is not divided into sections, ask the children to group some of the items in it.

   c. List the groups on a sheet of paper.

   d. Cut out or draw pictures of the items in the catalog which would fit into each group.

Activity 8

Grouping Manipulatives

Along with the catalog activities, use the many manipulatives available around the house or for sale to help the children group objects. Keys, sea shells, rocks, buttons, different sizes of bottle caps, lids, or any group of objects which can be sorted in more than one way can be used.

Keys

1. Collect as many old keys as possible (house, car, office, and so on) and examine them.

2. Note major differences: rounded, squared, or other-shaped tops; one or two holes; long or short; many or few notches.

3. Ask the children to divide the keys according to the groups chosen.

4. If they grasp these differences, ask them to think of more complex groups based on two or more features from their first observations. For example, square top keys with one hole, long keys with round tops, or similar variations.

5. For children who have no difficulty with the previous activities, take the activity one step further and ask them to find keys which can fit in more than one group or in overlapping groups. Use string or yarn circles to make the overlapping of the groups clear.

Buttons

1. Randomly select a handful of buttons and have the children look at them carefully.

2. Let them identify and show different ways to divide the buttons: by color, shape, size, the number of holes, and the type of fastener.

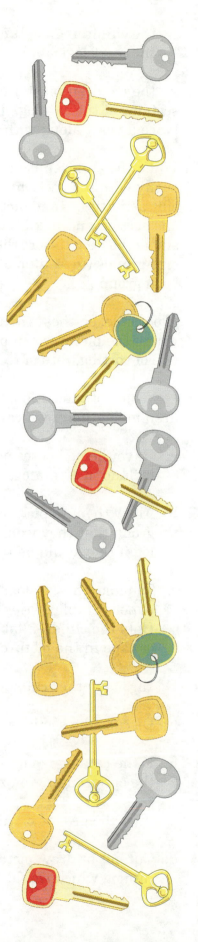

3. Have the children divide the buttons into groups one at a time.

4. Ask them to explain how one button can fit into more than one group depending on the way in which the buttons are divided. A small, square, blue button with two holes can fit into groups for: small buttons, square buttons, blue buttons, and two-holed buttons.

5. For a more difficult activity for those who can grasp it, have the children find overlapping groups for the buttons. Use string or yarn circles to help the children "see" the overlapping of the groups.

Additional grouping ideas

Many things can be grouped using the steps given for keys and buttons. Let the children help find other items which can be grouped in more than one way. Use materials and activities at hand around the house. For example, let the children help with the laundry.

1. As the children help sort the laundry for washing, talk to them about how and why it is sorted as it is: light clothes, dark clothes, delicate fabrics, and heavier fabrics.

2. When the laundry is finished and ready to fold, introduce them to different types of sorting.

   a. Have the children find all of the socks and sort them into pairs.

   b. Then have them sort them by "person."

3. Choose different items to sort each time such as T-shirts, towels, shorts, or shirts.

4. Have the children think of ways to sort the clothes such as color, size, or the person to whom the clothes belong.

5. Ask them if they can think of ways in which some items fit into more than one group.

Activity 9

Grouping By Senses

Another variation in grouping can be done by using the senses.

1. Place several items on the table which can be grouped by taste such as sweet, sour, salty, or by touch such as soft, rough, smooth, sharp.

2. Have the children group the items first by general category of taste and touch, then within the groups of sweet, sour, salty; rough, smooth, soft, sharp. Let them close their eyes and feel the objects in the "touch" group.

3. Have the children think of other things that would fit into each of the groups.

4. Document the groups in a book or make a collage or mobile of the things in each group.

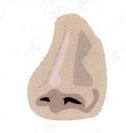

5. When they have done the initial catagorizing and have no difficulty in adding to the groups, move on to the other senses.

    a. the children what their other senses can tell them about the objects in the general groups. Can they smell the objects as well as taste them? Can they see that a stuffed animal is soft or that scissors are sharp? Can they hear a ball bounce and see that it is smooth?

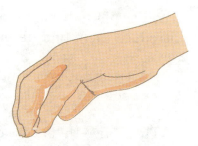

    b. Have the children redivide the objects by the senses of smell, sight, and hearing. Then ask them to find or think of other items for each of these new groups.

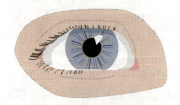

    c. Document these sense groups in a book, collage, or mobile.

6. Ask the children to think about the objects and name some which can be placed in more than one group. Are any in overlapping groups?

Further Practice

Make or purchase workbooks or worksheets which extend these grouping activities.

As stated earlier, matching, one-to-one correspondence, and grouping are very important skills which the children will need to be successful in school. Not all children will be ready for all of the activities in this section. Let the children go as far as they are able easily and naturally.

As always, and particularly in this section, use whatever means are available to reinforce the concepts. Everything and everyone fits into several groups (categories). Remember that there are many, many learning opportunities in the children's world.

Advanced Preschool

The next two chapters mark a distinct increase in the diffuculty of the activites. It is not advisable to intermix activities from the next two chapters with previous ones until the children have either worked their way through most of the previous chapters or are preparing to enter kindergarten. A familiarization with what the chapters contain is all that is necessary. Mastery of these concepts should take place in a quality kindergarten program when the child is older.

168

Section 6–Language Readiness

Introduction

Language readiness starts as soon as children begin to respond to the language of those around them. Preparing children to read can take on many forms. Nothing, perhaps, is more controversial than a position on when and how children should learn to read. This text is not meant to take up these arguments. Rather, it is a guide to readiness for the disciplines required for children to enter a more formal learning atmosphere. In this section ideas for reading *readiness* will be presented. This is *not* a specific program for teaching children to read. Parents and preschool teachers will be the best judges of children's readiness to begin a formal reading program. For some children this will happen early. For others it may take until the age of seven or eight before they can handle all of the skills needed for being a successful reader.

The following activities from previous sections relate to this section: *Color Section* Activities Four, Eight, Thirteen, Fourteen, and Seventeen; *Shape Section* Activities Fourteen, Eighteen, and Nineteen; *Size Section* Activities Eight and Sixteen; and *Position and Direction Section* Activities One, Two, Three, Eleven, Thirteen, Sixteen, Seventeen, Nineteen, Twenty, Twenty-Two, Twenty-Three, Twenty-Five, Twenty-Seven, Twenty-Nine, Thirty-Two through Thirty-Eight, Forty-Two, and Forty-Three.

The language readiness areas covered in the following activities are listening, letter recognition, sound recognition, word recognition, and comprehension. This is not a reading program, but a pre-reading program. If the children master all of the activities here and throughout the book they may very well be ready to read. Preview the section. Read through the activities and pick those which suit the children's needs at the time. If the children are ready for an activity, proceed. If they have great difficulty or become very tired after trying their best, put the activity aside for another day. Review materials which will help the children move more easily into the difficult activity.

In the area of reading readiness, many good workbooks are also available commercially either in department stores or teaching materials' stores. These are generally graded Preschool, Kindergarten, First Grade, etc. It is recommended that you look at the book before you buy it to see if the book is suitable for your children's level.

Activity 1

Talk to Children

Talking to children teaches them to listen.

1. From the very beginning use complete sentences, naming objects, colors, and specific characteristics whenever possible. Never use "baby talk."

2. As children begin to comprehend more, use the time together to observe and talk about the world, their home, church, stores, or nature.

3. Introduce distinctions into the conversation. "That building is taller than daddy." "That dog is shorter than you are." "Walk in front of me." "Walk beside me." "See how high the bird can fly."

4. All of this talk and observation should strengthen the children's listening skills and in turn their learning.

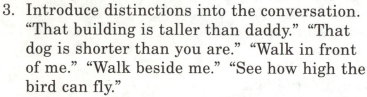

Activity 2

Read to Children

Read! Read! Read! Children will benefit from exposure to reading at a very early age.

1. Read every day even if only for a short time.

2. Read storybooks, picture books, poetry, and songs. This strengthens listening skills, a desire to read, and an "ear" for the language. Children must have these to be successful in reading and writing.

3. As soon as the children become interested in books, begin to show them that the book is read from left to right. Take them to the library and look at books with them. Check for story hours. Many libraries now have story times for parents and toddlers together.

4. Have the children act out scenes or short stories to enhance their vocabulary and comprehension skills. Encourage them to create and act out their own stories as well.

Activity 3

Beginning Writing

As an introduction to writing, let young children experiment with crayons by drawing flowing circles and lines.

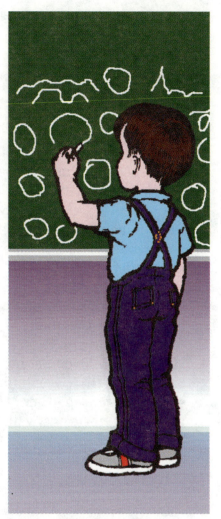

1. Do not begin formal writing activities until the children have the proper coordination skills. The children need the proper eye-hand coordination and fine motor skills to hold the pencil correctly and to form words. If the children have difficulties, do some simple exercises with them. Do not force them to do something they simply are not physically ready to do.

2. If the children are eager to write:

   a. Guide them in the proper way to hold the pencil.

   b. Remind them that writing is done from the left side of the page to the right side. Demonstrate this for them.

   c. From the very beginning, show them the correct way to form letters. Be sure they do not develop bad writing habits. They will be difficult to correct later.

   d. Select the writing style or program which the children will be using in school or at home and follow through with that program so that the children will not be confused.

   e. Help the children finish words, sentences, or activities which are difficult for them.

   f. *Praise all efforts.*

Activity 4

Listening

Reading to the children, giving them simple directions, listening to music, and learning songs and nursery rhymes help to build listening skills. These activities should be a part of the children's experience from birth. In preparation for kindergarten, some specific listening activities can be introduced.

1. When giving a direction to children, keep it simple and do not repeat it. This will teach them to listen the first time a direction is given and to ask questions only if the direction is not clearly understood.

2. Do some simple pattern drills with the children.

   a. Say a set of three words and have the children repeat them. Increase the number of words as the children are able.

      1) bear, doll, car

      2) door, window, carpet

      3) head, hand, hear

   b. Give the children simple sentences to repeat. Gradually make the sentences longer. See Jill run and play. Jan's ball is red, green, and white. Amelia likes stories about cowboys.

   c. Clap a pattern for the children to repeat. Begin with a simple pattern and gradually make it more complicated.

      Simple Pattern

      1) *Clap* pause *clap* pause *clap*

      2) *Clap clap* pause *clap* pause *clap*

      3) *Clap clap* pause *clap clap* pause *clap*

      4) *Clap clap* pause *clap* pause *clap clap*

Once upon a time in a far away land, there lived a handsome young prince who was very, very brave. He had all of the wonderful things a young man could ever wish for except for real happiness and

Complex Pattern

1) *Clap clap clap* pause *clap clap* pause *clap* pause *clap clap*

2) *Clap* pause *clap clap clap* pause *clap* pause *clap clap*

3) *Clap clap* pause *clap clap clap* pause *clap clap* pause *clap clap clap*

4) *Clap* pause *clap clap* pause *clap* pause *clap clap* pause *clap*

d. Extend the clapping pattern to words and names to get the children used to the sound and rhythm of the language.

1) John
   clap

2) E - liz - a - beth
   clap   clap   clap   clap

3) Ro - bert
   clap   clap

4) Jer - e - my
   clap   clap   clap

5) Ma -ry had a lit - tle lamb
   clap   clap clap clap clap   clap   clap

3. Play musical games.

a. Ask the children to either walk, march, skip, or jump to music. Check to see if they are listening to the rhythm of the music or just moving to their own rhythm.

b. Stop the music and have the children stop or "freeze" in place.

c. Ask the children to clap or snap their fingers to the rhythm of the music.

4. Listen to the sounds of the language.

   a. Have the children listen for one sound at a time. Have a "t" day in which they become conscious of the times they hear, say, or see the letter "t." This is good preparation for identifying the beginning, middle, and final sounds later.

   b. Tune the children's ears to rhyming sounds. Listen for them in nursery rhymes, poetry, songs, etc.

5. Have the children "tune in" on the sounds around them.

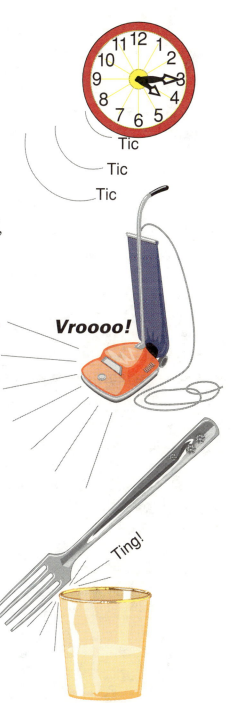

   a. Tell them to close their eyes and listen to the sounds in the room, in the yard, and in the car.

   b. Make a chart or book of sounds for different areas such as nature sounds, kitchen sounds, and car sounds.

   c. Blindfold the children and make different sounds (clap, stomp, sing, drum) from different parts of the room. See if they can identify in what part of the room the sound originates and what the sound is.

175

Activity 5

Letter Recognition

Children need to recognize the letters of the alphabet before they can read. Do simple letter-recognition activities to strengthen this skill.

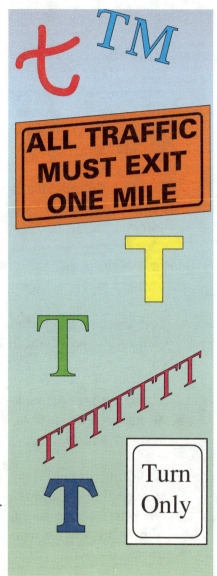

1. The children will have learned certain letters in the course of learning colors, shapes, sizes, and directions. Begin with the letters they already know. Most children should already know the letters in their own names.

2. Play simple matching games with letter flash cards. Begin with matching small letters to small letters and capital letters to capital letters. Proceed to matching capital and small letters when the children are familiar with both forms of the same letter. Say the name of each letter as it is matched.

3. Have a day for each letter. If the letter for the day is "t," have the children look and listen for "t." They can look for the letter "t" around the house, in the store, on signs or billboards, in catalogs, on books or magazines, etc.

4. Have them make the letters from clay, yarn, play dough, or pipe cleaners.

5. Use letter recognition worksheets, or hidden letter sheets to reinforce the skill (see illustration).

6. On large tag board or heavy paper, make an alphabet chart with a large square around each letter. Place the chart on the floor. Have the children toss a ring, bean bag, or coin onto the chart and name the letter in the square.

7. Play other flash card games. Hold up a card. Ask a child to name the letter. If the card is named correctly, the child can collect the card. The winner is the one with the most cards.

8. Have the children think of games or other ways to help them learn and remember the letters.

Activity 6

Sound Recognition

As children learn the letters, point out to them that each letter has a name, just as they have names. Tell them that the name of the letter is not always the sound which the letter makes. Sound recognition is tied very closely to the listening skills. To read, they will have to make the connections between the sounds they hear and the sounds which the letters represent.

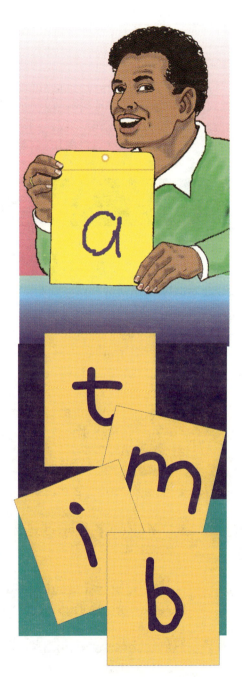

1. Work on one sound at a time. First pick easy sounds such as b, d, t, s, and f.

2. Listen to the sound.

3 Now look at the letter which makes that sound.

4. Tie the activity in with the listening and recognition exercises for the "sound of the day" ideas in *Activity One* and *Two*.

5. Practice using the sound. Start with the letter "t." Follow the same activities as new sounds are introduced.

   a. Make a set of cards for each sound. Self adhesive note sheets work well.

   b. Help the children to find things which have the same sound as at the beginning of their names. If they are working on sound and recognition of the letter "t," have them find things which have the "t" sound at the beginning of the word such as table, towel, toy, or top. Let them take a letter card with a "t" printed on it and attach it to the objects which begin with the "t" sound. Leave the letters in place for several days, even after moving on to a new sound.

   c. Make a large envelope for each sound. Collect pictures and words which begin with the "t" sound. Place the pictures and words in the envelope and review them often.

d. Booklets can be made for each sound. Find or draw pictures and words which begin with the sound and place them in the booklet.

e. As children progress with the beginning sounds and have little difficulty, move on to ending sounds using the same steps of labeling and making files or booklets.

f. After they become very proficient with beginning and ending sounds, try introducing middle sounds (those heard in the middle of a word such as ha**pp**y, li**tt**le, la**dd**er).

Activity 7

Rhyming

Children have been exposed to rhymes from birth if their parents have read rhymes or poems and sung songs to them. They love to play rhyming games and make up silly songs and poems. Building on this love is a big step towards reading.

1. Read to the children their favorite nursery rhymes. Ask them to repeat the rhyming words after you.

2. Play rhyming games with the children.

   a. Make up two sentences omitting the final word.

      "Oh, how I would like to be,
      Swinging high up in a _____."

Have the children finish the sentence. Accept whatever the children say as long as the final word rhymes with "be." These rhymes do not have to make "sense." Choose ending words which have a variety of rhyming possibilities. Here are some other sample rhyme starters:

   "One day I saw a funny cat
   Who ran and chased a big black ____."

178

"There once was a silly man
Who drove to work in a great, big _____."

"In a house lived a little bug
Who curled up in a small green _____."

"I saw a flower of deepest blue
Now I want to give it to _____."

When they can complete the sentences easily,
see if they can make up their own second line.

b. Have the children begin to collect pictures which
they have cut out or drawn and words which
rhyme. This introduces the children to rhyming
families. Note here that all words which rhyme
are *not* spelled the same way. The children do
not need to deal with this now.

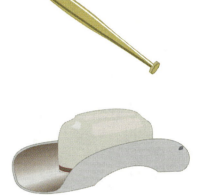

at: cat, hat, mat, sat, bat, fat, pat, rat, vat, that
an: can, fan, man, pan, ran, tan, van
ed: bed, dead, fed, head, led, Ned, red, said, Ted
ug: bug, jug, lug, mug, pug, rug, tug
un: bun, done, fun, pun, run, sun, ton, won
I: buy, bye, by, dye, die, hi, high, my, pie, rye

c. Have the children look for things whose names
rhyme. Have them look around the house, at
the store, in school, at church, and as they ride
to and from places.

d. Teach them jump rope rhymes.

e. Give them a set of three words (two which
rhyme, one which does not). Ask them to pick
only the rhyming words. Example: bed, red,
box; door, house, floor; run, tree, sun.

f. Provide workbook pages which have the children match rhyming pictures.

g. When the children are progressing, provide
workbook pages which have the children select
rhyming pairs from sets of three (two rhyming,
and one not).

h. Have them make rhyming charts or booklets.

179

Activity 8

Word Recognition

Children will begin recognizing certain words early. As soon as they show an interest in seeing or "reading" written words, help and encourage them by introducing them to the words. Most children are interested in seeing their names printed out. They may also be interested in the names of colors and shapes, favorite pets or toys, the names of family members, and the titles of stories they have composed.

1. When the children become interested in reading, or display the ability to recognize letters, sounds, and basic words, begin showing them how words are made up of certain sounds.

2. Help them to sound out the words they want to know.

3. Write the words for different things in the house or classroom on a set of cards and make a duplicate set. Attach one set of the cards to the objects. Give the cards from the other set to the children as they search out the objects with the matching words.

4. Help them start a list of words that they know.

5. Have the children search for words they know in magazines and catalogs.

6. Use easy workbook pages to strengthen word recognition and to introduce new, related words.

7. Build on the rhyming activity by showing the children how new words can be made by changing the first letter sound.

8. Have them make up their own stories or poems. Write out the stories and read them to the children.

Activity 9

Comprehension

Comprehension exercises check and enhance the children's understanding of the language as it is used in speech and stories. This is essential for reading.

1. After the children have listened to a story, ask them questions to check their understanding of the story. "What was the story about?" "Who were the main characters?" "What happened at the beginning, middle, and end of the story?"

2. Tell the children only the beginning or the ending of a story. Let them provide the rest.

3. Make up stories from pictures which interest them. Ask what they see in the picture. "What might have happened before and after the picture took place?" Have them describe parts of the picture using color and action words.

4. Cut story strips apart, such as in the comics section of the paper. Ask the children to put the story in the correct order.

5. Find examples in workbooks or make up picture sets which can be put in a first, next, and last order. Use pictures of a mother and child mixing up a cake, putting it in the oven, decorating, and eating the cake. Have them put the pictures in order. Have them make up a story for the pictures they put in order.

6. Read a story to the children and ask them to draw a picture of the things they remember about the story.

7. Purchase or make puppets of all kinds (hand, stocking, and string stick). Let the children use them to retell a story or to create a beginning or ending for stories. Puppets may be used throughout the book to reinforce concepts.

Be alert and use the many opportunities that arise each day to help children prepare for reading.

Section 7–Math Readiness

Introduction

Many sections of this book have already covered concepts needed for understanding math. Mastery of the concepts in the sections on shapes, size, and especially matching and grouping will give a good foundation. More specific areas which can be covered before children go to kindergarten are: counting, number recognition, tallying, greater than and less than, time, weight, measurement, and money. All of the required skills can be taught at home with a minimum of investment. Most materials can be found around the house. In all subjects drill periods, not games, should be controlled to about ten minutes per year of age. For instance, a four-year-old should not be required to drill on math more than forty minutes a day. Math games could be played much longer, if the children enjoy them.

Remember the activities in this section are suggestions for introducing math skills. Introduce the activities at a rate the children can handle. If they do not readily catch on to certain skills, move on to others. Many of the skills will be covered in kindergarten. Do not push children who have difficulty with any or all of this section.

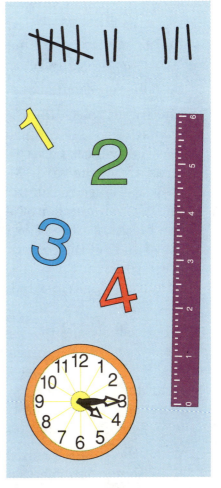

Review activities from previous sections if needed. The following activities relate to this section:

Section 1–Color: Activity Nineteen
Section 2–Shape: Activities Two, Three, Eleven, Thirteen, Fifteen, Sixteen, Twenty, and Twenty-Three
Section 3–Size: Activities Three through Seven, Nine, Seventeen, Nineteen, Twenty, Twenty-One, and Twenty-Three
Section 4–Position and Direction: Activities Four, Fifteen, Thirty-One, Thirty-Four, Forty-Two, and Forty-Three
Section 5–Matching and Grouping: All Activities

Activity 1

Counting

1. From the very beginning, count small groups of objects *for* the children.

2 Second, you should count the objects *with* them.

3. Finally, let the children count the objects *for themselves*. This can be as simple as counting how many blocks are in a tower or how many birds are in the yard. Make a game of it and they will learn to count naturally. Have them find a given number of objects: ten crayons, five blocks, six bears, or three pencils. When they can find the correct number of objects every time, let them be the "caller" and ask the parent or older child to find a certain number of objects.

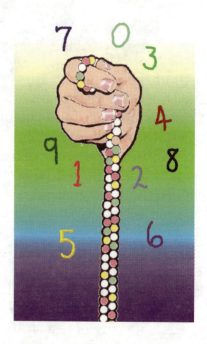

4. Progressively add five more objects to the counting sequence until the children have difficulty counting. For example, when they can easily count ten objects, add five more. Many children can easily learn to count to one hundred this way if counting is approached in stages.

5. When the children can count to twenty easily, show them that objects can be divided into groups to make counting easier and quicker. Use blocks, bears, or other manipulatives.

   a. Have the children take ten blocks and ask them to sort the blocks into groups which have the same number in each group. Let them experiment until they figure out that ten can be divided in two ways, by twos and by fives. Help them only if they have difficulty after several tries.

   b. If the children grasp this concept, move on to fifteen blocks. Let them find the natural groupings for fifteen (threes and fives).

   c. Continue to move on to twenty, twenty-five, and thirty as long as the children are able to do so.

6. When the children grasp the grouping of the blocks, talk to them about counting by fives, tens, and twos. Recite the numbers used in counting by fives and ask the children to repeat the numbers. Let them show these counting groups with their blocks. Repeat the same procedure for tens and twos.

7. Have the children count wherever they are. They can count boxes at the grocery store, people and trees in the park, flowers in the garden, or other groups.

8. If the group they wish to count is large, ask them if they can think of easier ways to count the people or to keep track of the number.

   a. They may choose to count by twos or fives if they are able.

   b. They can be taught to tally the number of objects. Begin with a small number of objects. Many easy math workbooks have pages which require a tally to record the number in a set.

      1) Place four buttons on the table.

      2) On a chalkboard or piece of paper, show the children how to record the number as they count. ////

      3) Give them several turns until they realize that one "/" stands for one object.

      4) When recording up to four objects is mastered, show them how to record five. ⑅ This requires more practice.

      5) If the children master this, go on to the six through nine object groups. ⑅ / ⑅ // ⑅ /// ⑅ ////

      6) See if the children can figure out how to tally ten. ⑅ ⑅

9. Another way to help the children tally and count by fives and tens is to give them popsicle (craft) sticks. Have them sort and bundle them with rubber bands or yarn into the desired groups. Let them practice other groupings as they are able.

185

Activity 2

Number Recognition

1. Make or purchase a set of number flash cards (one through fifty or one through one hundred).

2. When the children begin to count, place the number card next to the group.

3. Tell the children that the number stands for the number of objects in the group they have just counted.

4. Then write the number for the children so that they can begin to associate the written number with the number of objects in a group.

5. Make number flash card sets and number puzzles similar to the illustrations.

6. Go on a number hunt. Have the children look in magazines, catalogs, and newspapers for numbers to cut out.

7. Use the numbers they find to make a number book.

   a. Write or paste the number at the top of the page.

   b. Draw or paste the correct number of items on the page.

   c. Print the number word next to the number or at the bottom of the page.

8. Use treats (raisins, small crackers, etc.) for recognition practice. If the children can place the correct number of treats on the card, they are allowed to eat the treat.

9. Make or purchase worksheets which have color by number puzzle pages.

10. Choose worksheets which require the children to recognize the number and link it to a group of objects.

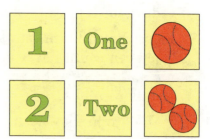

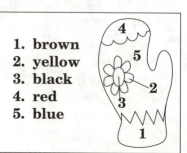

1. brown
2. yellow
3. black
4. red
5. blue

Activity 3

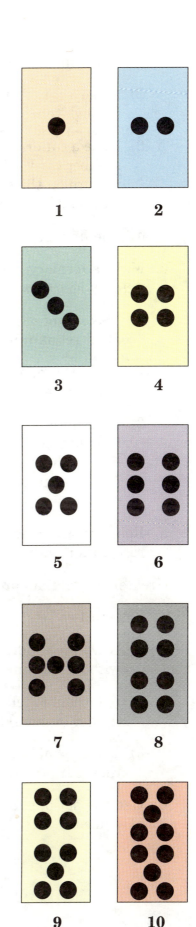

Sets

The children have been working with sets throughout this book. The term "set" is often used in mathematics texts and simply refers to a group or number of objects or people which have something in common. The children work with sets whenever they:

Sort a group of objects by color, shape, size, and common characteristics. All matching activities in the *Color*, *Shape*, and *Size Sections*, and especially the *Matching and Grouping Section Activities Five* through *Ten* would be helpful review for this.

Match something one-to-one (see *Matching and Grouping Section Activities Three* and *Four*).

Arrange items from smallest to largest, largest to smallest, or in first, second, and third order.

Reviewing any or all of these activities will reinforce the children's understanding of sets and help them to recognize a set which stands for a specific number of items.

1. Make cards for the number groups from one to ten. These can be simple dot patterns found on dominoes or pictures drawn or cut from a magazine.

2. Set games.

   a. Play dominoes.

   b. Make or purchase other games which will help the children to identify a certain pattern with a given number.

   c. Make a bingo or lotto style game using at least six different sets of patterns to give you six player cards (see instructions in the *Color Section Activity Thirteen*).

187

1) Draw a number pattern in each of the six boxes on each card (see illustration)

2) Make a set of cards for the numbers one through ten.

3) Have a caller or one of the children pick a number card. If it matches a number pattern on the card, they can place a marker on the space.

4) The first child to fill a card is the winner.

d. Make a memory game as in *Color Section Activity Fourteen*.

1) Make a set of pattern cards and an equivalent set of number cards.

2) Lay all cards face down on the table and play as other memory games.

3) As children become more familiar with the number words, make a third set with the number words and add to the game. Accept a match of: number and pattern, number and word, or pattern and word.

e. Reinforce the concepts of sets and pattern recognition with workbook activities.

3. Greater (more) than and less than.

a. Lay out two sets of objects on the table.

1). Have the children look at the two sets without touching them or counting them.

2) Ask them to tell which set is greater (larger or more) than the other.

3) Let the children count the sets to see if they were correct.

b. Use the set of cards from the previous exercises.

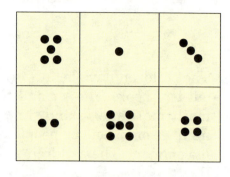

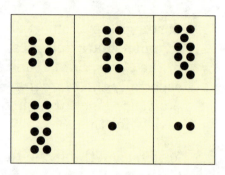

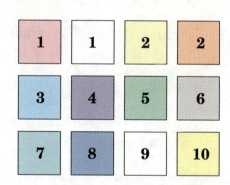

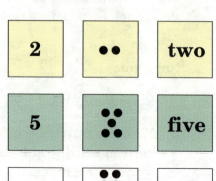

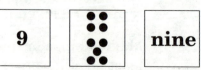

1) Lay these cards face up on the table in sets of two. Do not have matching sets, such as two twos.

2) Help the children select the one in the first set that is less than the other.

3) Ask them to choose the one in the second set that is greater.

4) Continue through all the sets requesting the children to tell whether the number is greater or less than the other number in the set.

5) When the children progress satisfactorily, have them lay out the sets and ask another child or an adult to select the card that is greater or less than the other card.

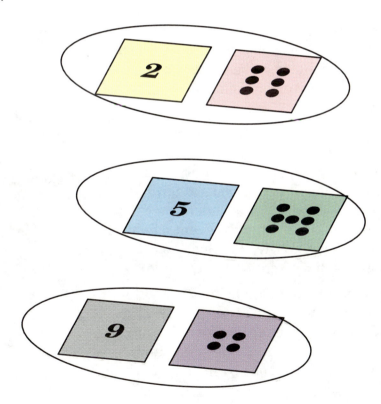

Activity 4

Time

Understanding and telling time can be very difficult for children if it is not approached regularly and simply from the time children are very young. Calendars and clocks are two types of devices used to measure time. Familiarizing children from an early age with both means of measuring time will make the formal learning of both much easier. The following suggestions are designed to increase the children's understanding and time telling skills with both calendars and clocks.

Calendars

1. Make or purchase a large calendar which can be used over again (size about 18" x 25"). Some very good calendars are available commercially. They come with press-ons for special occasions, weather symbols, holiday stickers, and an erasable pencil for writing appointments and special messages.

2. To keep a record of the year's events for the children, purchase or make a large calendar which allows you to write in the month and the numbers. Such calendars can be found in office supply stores. As children grow older, the calendar can be used to trace different events, field trips, or special days. Write stories or do art projects from the diary kept on the calendar.

3. Make a set of numbers that can be attached to the calendar for each month. Add the new number each day. When the children are old enough, have them say the number as it is added and count the days that have gone by in the month.

4. Make a set of names using each month of the year. Attach the correct name to the calendar each month.

5. When the children are very young, use the calendar to track the days. This can be done very simply by charting the weather each day. Make several brightly colored symbols for sunny, rainy,

190

cloudy, partly cloudy, and snowy days. With a pin or paper clip, attach the symbol for the day's weather. If the weather changes during the day add another symbol. When the children are old enough, talk about how the calendar shows the progression of days through a month.

6. Mark special days, holidays, family birthdays, or special trips, so that the children have something to look forward to. Count with the children the number of days remaining until these events.

7. Make or purchase a special activity calendar for the year. This type of calendar has a simple activity, game, or song for each day of the year. Several companies have these on the market for preschoolers. *Growing Child* prints one in each month's newsletter (see page 8).

If children grow up with the sense of the progression of days, weeks, or months, they will not have difficulty when they are faced with "learning" to read the calendar in school.

Clocks

Another way to measure time is a clock. Children grow up in a world surrounded by all kinds of clocks. Using the clocks and talking with the children about time when they are young will build the base for learning to tell time when they come to it in school.

1. Have at least two clocks in the house which have "hands" and "faces." Simple clocks with large numbers are the best. Digital clocks teach children to read numbers, but do not teach them to tell time or to understand the progression of time.

2. When the children are very young, use the clock to show them when something important will happen on a particular day. If a trip to the park is planned, point to the clock and show them where the hands of the clock will be when it is time to leave. You may want to draw a clock on a sheet of paper showing the time to leave so that they can compare it to the clock.

3. Call attention to things which happen at nearly the same time each day: breakfast, lunch, din-

ner, bedtime, going to work, and coming home from work. By doing this each day, the children begin to recognize the times when events happen. They begin to observe a progression of time through a day.

4. When the children are older, make a paper plate clock with them.

   a. Write the numbers from one to twelve on a paper plate as on a clock. Make a large and a small hand and attach them in the center with a brad.

   b. Use the clock to help the children learn how a clock functions. Set the hands of the clock and have them compare it with the real clock.

   c. When doing "Hickory, Dickory, Dock," use this clock to see if the children can mark the times in the rhyme.

5. Have the children make a clock book.

   a. Talk about the different types of clocks children may see such as an alarm clock, wall clock, grandfather clock, watches (pocket and wrist), clock radios, tower clocks on buildings or churches, and digital clocks on appliances.

   b. Have them search the house or classroom to find different types of clocks. Look through catalogs, magazines, and newspapers.

   c. Cut out or draw pictures of different clocks and make a booklet.

6. When the children become seriously interested in telling time, make or purchase a good teaching clock which has the time in five minute segments written outside the numbers. These marks will help the children grasp the concept of five minute increments of time. Practice counting by fives to sixty with the children.

7. Purchase a good workbook on time, or make up some worksheets with blank clocks (no hands, just numbers) and help the children first draw the time for the hours, then the half-hours. Continue to use the paper plate clock to teach them to tell time.

Activity 5

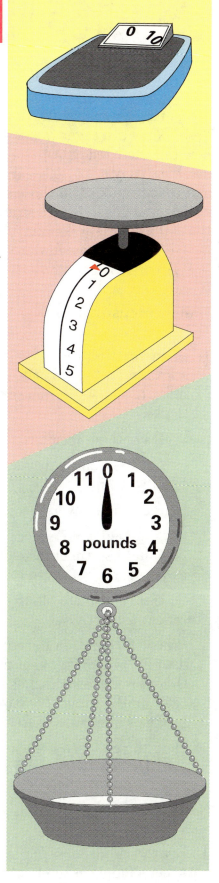

Weight

Helping children understand weight is easy if you answer their natural questions.

1. Begin by talking about how heavy or light an object feels to the children.

2. When the children ask how to tell the weight of an object, simply use a bathroom scale (not digital) to show them how the weight is recorded. They will delight in finding all sorts of things to weigh.

3. Have them use a kitchen scale for lighter objects.

4. Talk about the differences in the two types of scales: bathroom scales mark only half pounds and kitchen scales mark fractional parts of pounds as well as pounds.

5. Let them experiment in the produce section of the grocery store. If they want apples for their lunches, let them put some apples in a bag, guess how much they think it will weigh, and then check their guesses on the scale. Their estimates become more realistic the more practice they get. It makes shopping time a little longer, but it is worth the effort.

6. Let the children keep a record of their weight from one month to the next.

7. If the opportunity presents itself, show them the types of scales still used in some businesses which require weights and balances to give an accurate reading.

Activity 6

Measurement

Measuring things is also of great interest to children. They are eager to know how tall they are, how tall their teddy bears are, how long their beds are, etc. They are also eager to help in the kitchen and to learn about all those special measuring spoons and cups. Before starting these activities, the children might benefit from a review of the measuring activities in the *Size Section Activities Six, Twenty-One,* and *Twenty-Three.*

Linear Measurement

1. Show the children a twelve inch ruler, a yard stick, and a tape measure. Let them experiment to see which measuring device they need to use.

   a. Have them measure their own height.

   b. Let them measure how tall the kitchen table is.

   c. Pick some favorite toys to measure.

2. Give the children a piece of string twelve inches long and ask them to see how many objects they can find that measure twelve inches in length.

3. Give them a piece of string six inches long and repeat the activity.

4. When the children have done these activities for a while, ask them to select some objects that they think are six inches in length and bring them to the table. Measure the objects and see how close their estimates come.

5. Help the children keep a log of how tall they are. Update this every month or two.

Solid and Liquid Measurement

1. Let the children examine measuring cups and spoons found in the kitchen.

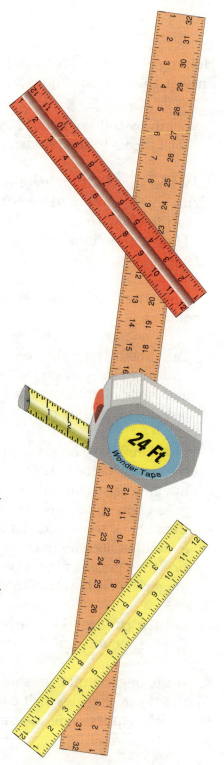

194

2. Have them use the sink or a large bowl of water to experiment with the cups and spoons and answer the following questions:

   a. How many one-fourth cups does it take to fill one cup?

   b. How many one-half cups are needed to fill a cup?

   c. What happens if they try to pour one cup of water into a half cup measure?

   d. How many one-fourth teaspoons does it take to fill a teaspoon? a tablespoon?

   e. How many one-half teaspoons does it take to fill a teaspoon? a tablespoon?

   f. It takes how many teaspoons to fill a tablespoon?

3. As they experiment, point to the fractions one-half and one-fourth. Ask them which one holds more (one-half).

4. After they have experimented, let them begin to help with the baking and cooking. Read the recipe to them one ingredient at a time. Let them find the correct cup or spoon and help measure the ingredient. As they watch a recipe develop, ask them what would happen if the measurements were wrong (too much liquid or not enough liquid).

5. Do an experiment with popcorn. Let the children measure out one-half cup of dry popcorn. After the corn is popped, have the children measure the results. They will be amazed at the difference.

Temperature

Thermometers are a method of measuring heat and cold. The children will remember having their temperatures taken. Do some simple experiments with thermometers to demonstrate this.

1. Take the children's temperature with a mercury thermometer. Show them the temperature reading.

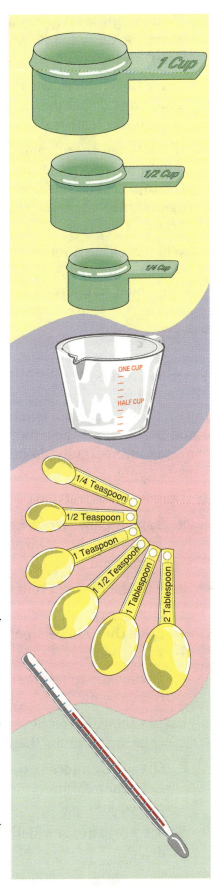

2. Find an outdoor thermometer and help them chart the daily temperatures. Check morning, noon, and early evening temperatures.

3. Show the children the thermostat on the air conditioning or heat pump in the house. Help them to read the temperature.

4. If a kitchen thermometer is available (candy or meat), measure the temperature of water from the tap. Then heat it slightly and measure again. Supervise the children at all times around the stove.

5. When cooking a roast or candy, let the children observe the temperature changes but stress that they must not get too close to the heat.

Fractions

Fractions can be taught in the cooking process. Measuring cups and spoons are divided into fractions. Food is cut into fractions so that all get equal portions. If the children do not grasp these concepts immediately, do not be concerned. Come back to them later.

1. Demonstrate fractions.

    a. Take a paper circle about the size of a pie and show the children how to divide it in half (two equal parts).

    b. Cut the circle in half and label each half.

    c. Cut many half circles of different sizes and have the children make collages or pictures with them.

    d. Demonstrate one-fourth in the same way you did one-half.

    e. Let the children help divide the next pie, cake, or pizza for the family meal.

    f. Give the children cupcakes to divide in half. Let other children judge whether the parts are equal.

2. Select worksheets which will reinforce these skills.

Activity 7

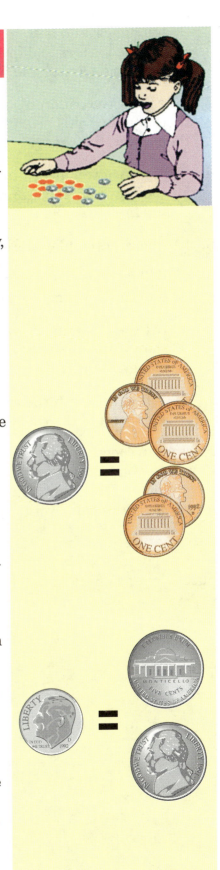

Money

A final area where children often have difficulty in math is money. This is another area where the difficulty can be greatly diminished if they are given opportunities to deal with money naturally.

1. When the children become curious about money, lay out an assortment of coins (pennies, nickels, dimes, and quarters). Treat this as a simple sorting exercise. Have them sort the coins (by color, by size, by the picture on the front, or by the picture on the back).

2. Begin to tell the children the distinctions between the coins.

   a. Show them that pennies count for one. Have them count ten pennies.

   b. When they grasp this concept, show them that one nickel equals the same amount as five pennies. Have them match several sets of five pennies to one nickel.

   c. If the children are progressing without difficulty, show them that one dime equals the same amount as ten pennies or two nickels. Let them work on one concept at a time, first matching ten pennies to one dime, then matching two nickels to one dime.

   d. As they progress with these activities, tie in the concepts with the counting activities. Count pennies by ones. Count nickels by fives. Count dimes by tens.

   e. If they advance beyond this stage, introduce the combinations which make a quarter (twenty-five pennies, five nickels, two dimes and one nickel).

   f. Some children may grasp all of this and be ready to move on to the combinations for one dollar (one hundred pennies, twenty nickels, ten dimes, and four quarters). Do not be alarmed if most children do not go beyond counting pennies and nickels.

3. Whenever the children go along shopping, let them see the coins given back in change. Help them count the change.

4. If they are given money to spend, let them pay for their own purchase and receive their own change.

5. Let the children play store.

    a. Collect empty cereal boxes and other product containers which can be easily cleaned.

    b. Let the children set up shop, set prices, and shop with play money. Make sure the play money is a close facsimile of the real thing.

    c. Take turns with the children playing the shopper and the cashier.

Most math concepts can be learned through natural processes. Make them a part of the every day life of the children. They can be strengthened by more formal activities from workbooks.

Use whatever is at hand. Don't miss opportunities which may take a few minutes longer, but will produce a lasting effect educationally.

MATERIALS LIST

The materials listed in this section can either be found around the house or purchased inexpensively. These lists are only a guide and idea starter. *No one needs everything in these lists.* Use whatever you have at hand or whatever you can obtain easily. Many stores are willing to give you samples or remnants. Others will ask a small fee for these items. Many games can be made from things at home. Please feel free to add items and to use these materials for other projects throughout the book. Most items may be listed in more than one section.

CAUTION: Some objects may be too small for very young children. Be very careful to choose objects which are appropriate for the age and the maturity of the child.

Art Supplies

Boxes
Cardboard
Calendars with large pictures
Catalogs
Clay
Clothes – may also be used for dress-up
Chalkboard and chalk
Colored paper
Colored pipe cleaners
Computer paper
Construction paper
Cotton balls
Crayons
Drawing paper – newsprint, manilla, etc.
Easel
Foam or sponge
Food coloring
Greeting cards
Junk mail
Magazines
Markers – washable
Newspapers

Paint – tempera, finger, or watercolors
Paint brushes
Paper and fabric scraps
Paper plates and bags
Paste or glue
Plastic bottles and berry baskets
Popsicle sticks – also used for counting by fives and tens
Safety scissors – Buy left-handed scissors if the child is left handed.
Smocks
Sticks or hangers
String
Styrofoam® "popcorn" packing material
Toothbrushes – old ones for painting
Tubes from paper towels, bathroom tissue, and wrapping paper
Wallpaper books
Wood scraps
Wrapping paper
Yarn

Commercial Products

Bingo
Building blocks – of any kind
Flash cards – These may be numbers, alphabet, and initial sounds.
Shape games
Number pattern recognition games
Counting and visual discrimination games

Lotto
Memory games
Shape blocks or pattern blocks
Tangrams
Tape recorder – to record children's stories and sounds around you
Tinkertoys® – for older children

Materials for Games, Charts, and Books

Chart Rings
5" x 8" cards

Tagboard
3" x 5" cards

Materials for Multi-use

Lacing cards
Stencils for tracing
Flannel boards and figures

Jump ropes
Puzzles
Stacking cubes or dolls

Science and Math Items

Calendars with large squares
Corks
Funnels
Inexpensive mircroscope
Magnets
Magnifying glass
Measuring cups and spoons
Mirrors

Play money
Prisms and reflectors
Ruler, yard stick, and tape measure
Rubber bands
Scale
Scoops
Sifters or strainers

Sorting Materials

Beads
Beans, dried peas, rice
Blocks
Buttons
Caps from toothpaste, jars, and bottles
Cars, trucks, dolls, and other toys –
    also used in acting out
Clothespins
Coins – also make good game markers
Counting bears
Dominoes
Geoboards, rubber bands, pattern
    papers, and cards
Keys
Leaves
Marbles
Material scraps
Nuts, bolts, screws, and washers – can
    be used for one-to-one correspon-
    dence.

Pasta
Pattern cards
Pegboards and pegs
Pine cones
Plastic bowls and lids; pots and pans
    and lids – good for one-to-one cor-
    respondence.
Plastic bread bag closures – good
    game markers
Ribbon
Rocks, small stones, and pebbles
Seashells
Seeds
Shoes
Socks
Thread spools
Tiles – one inch square
Toothpicks

Sorting and Storage Containers

Aluminum pie tins and TV trays
Coffee cans
Egg cartons
Film containers
Frozen juice cans – can be used to demon-
    strate cylinders.

Jars
Microwave containers
Milk cartons
Muffin tins
Plastic bowls and lids
Styrofoam® trays